Tackling Environmental Problems with the Help of Behavioural Insights

OECD
BETTER POLICIES FOR BETTER LIVES

This work is published under the responsibility of the Secretary-General of the OECD. The opinions expressed and arguments employed herein do not necessarily reflect the official views of OECD member countries.

This document and any map included herein are without prejudice to the status of or sovereignty over any territory, to the delimitation of international frontiers and boundaries and to the name of any territory, city or area.

Please cite this publication as:
OECD (2017), *Tackling Environmental Problems with the Help of Behavioural Insights*, OECD Publishing, Paris.
http://dx.doi.org/10.1787/9789264273887-en

ISBN 978-92-64-27386-3 (print)
ISBN 978-92-64-27388-7 (PDF)

The statistical data for Israel are supplied by and under the responsibility of the relevant Israeli authorities. The use of such data by the OECD is without prejudice to the status of the Golan Heights, East Jerusalem and Israeli settlements in the West Bank under the terms of international law.

Photo credits: Cover © Myimagine/Shutterstock.com, © zentradyi3ell/Shutterstock.com.

Corrigenda to OECD publications may be found on line at: *www.oecd.org/about/publishing/corrigenda.htm*.

Foreword

Tackling environmental problems requires changing the behaviour of individuals, households, firms and governmental organisations. Policy can build on a diverse array of powerful instruments to green behaviour. Next to instruments traditionally used for this purpose, such as regulation, taxes, and tradable permits, *behavioural insights* are increasingly recognised as an important component of policy makers' toolbox to tackle environmental problems. Behavioural insights denote knowledge acquired from behavioural sciences, including behavioural economics, psychology and neuroscience. These insights can help policy makers obtain a deeper understanding of the behavioural mechanisms that contribute to environmental problems, and eventually design and implement more effective policy interventions.

The OECD Environment Directorate has conducted work on the use of behavioural insights in environmentally relevant policies since 2011. A wide spectrum of studies have previously been undertaken, ranging from reviews of the relevant academic literature, lab experiments to incentivise individuals to make more sustainable food choices, to in-house experiments to green default thermostat settings.

This report offers a different perspective on the analysis of the use of behavioural insights to tackle environmental problems. Motivated by the keen interest recently shown by many policy makers in applying behavioural insights to green consumption, investment and compliance decisions by individuals and firms, the report provides an up-to-date review of relevant interventions in OECD countries and beyond. The report analyses 36 such *behavioural interventions*, initiated by ministries and agencies responsible for environment and energy, as well as cross-government behavioural insights teams mainly between 2010 and 2016. It covers a variety of policy areas: energy, water and food consumption, transport and car choice, waste management and resource efficiency, and compliance with environmental regulation.

Information about the interventions analysed in this report was collected through: i) communications with country delegates to the OECD Working Party on Integrating Environmental and Economic Policies; ii) interviews with experts and practitioners from national and regional governments and the European Commission; and iii) desk research, based on the consultation of online databases, publications and other resources, including the websites of teams dedicated to the application of behavioural insights.

The report shows that behavioural interventions tackling environmental problems have pursued a broad range of objectives: i) encourage conservation of resources, such as energy, water and materials; ii) promote private investment in more efficient technologies; iii) incentivise environmentally sustainable consumption patterns; and iv) increase compliance with environmental regulation and participation in voluntary schemes, both on the side of individuals and firms. Examples of behavioural interventions range from the provision of timely feedback on the consumption and costs of everyday activities to conserve energy and water, to the framing of information in a way that is more easily understandable by consumers, and to the leverage of comparisons with relevant social groups to influence individual consumption and investment choices. Ultimately, the report reveals which interventions have proven to work – and which ones have not – in policy practice.

Acknowledgements

This report was authored by Elisabetta Cornago, Alexandros Dimitropoulos, Walid Oueslati and Shardul Agrawala of the Environment and Economy Integration Division of the OECD Environment Directorate. The authors are grateful to delegates to the OECD Working Party on Integrating Environmental and Economic Policies, who provided valuable input, comments and feedback on earlier drafts of the report.

The report benefitted from discussions with a number of representatives from national and regional governments and the European Commission. The authors of the report are grateful to: Naomi Boccola, Kevin Chadwick, Trish Lavery and Lani Perlesz (Department of the Environment and Energy, Australia), Shabnam Gill (Behavioural Insights Unit of New South Wales, Australia); Elizabeth Hardy (Privy Council's Innovation Hub, Canada); Xavier Troussard, Emanuele Ciriolo, François Dessart, Joana Sousa Lourenço, Sara Rafael Almeida and René van Bavel (Joint Research Centre, European Commission), Ewout Deurwaarder (DG Energy, European Commission); Valeriu-Dan Dionysie (DG Justice and Consumers, European Commission), Marilena Di Stasi (Consumers, Health, Agriculture and Food Executive Agency, European Commission); Magdalena Lazcano Maturana (SERNAC, Chile), Javier Assereto Cortés (Superintendencia de Electricidad y Combustibles, Chile); Françoise Waintrop (Secrétariat Général pour la Modernisation de l'Action Publique, France); Andrea Schneider (Office of the Federal Chancellor, Germany), Dirk Osiek (German Environment Agency); Yuval Laster and Opher Zylbertal (Israeli Ministry of Environmental Protection); Odette van de Riet (Ministry of Infrastructure and the Environment, the Netherlands); Susanna Fieber, Laura Platchkov and Alexandra Strauss (Federal Office for the Environment, Switzerland), Anne-Kathrin Faust (Federal Office of Energy, Switzerland); Elisabeth Costa and Katy King (Behavioural Insights Team, United Kingdom); Michael Hand (Social and Behavioral Sciences Team, United States); and Ammaarah Kamish (Western Cape Government, South Africa). Thanks are extended to Pelle Guldborg Hansen (Roskilde University and iNudgeYou) and Knut Ivar Karevold (GreeNudge), who contributed to a better understanding of the co-operation between governments, and academia and the private sector on the application of behavioural insights to policy making. The authors are also grateful to Faisal Naru and Filippo Cavassini (OECD Public Governance and Territorial Development Directorate), for stimulating discussions and feedback on the report.

Janine Treves provided guidance throughout the editorial process. Katjusha Boffa, Natasha Cline-Thomas, Beth Del Bourgo and Stéphanie Simonin-Edwards provided editorial assistance. Peter Vogelpoel did the typesetting.

The OECD Secretariat would like to gratefully acknowledge financial support for this work from the Department of the Environment and Energy, Australia, and the Federal Office for the Environment, Switzerland.

Table of contents

Figures

Tables

Boxes

Reader's guide

The objective of this report is twofold: first, to understand the extent to which behavioural insights are being incorporated in environmentally relevant policy making, as well as the outcomes of this process; and second, to provide policy makers with concrete examples of successful as well as unsuccessful applications of behavioural insights to the design and implementation of relevant policies.

This reader's guide presents all definitions of terms related to behavioural biases, interventions and levers, as well as those related to the methods used to test and assess the impact of behavioural interventions. While the definitions of these terms are also presented in Chapters 1 and 2, this guide mainly aims to support the reading of the chapters reviewing applications of behavioural insights to various policy areas: energy consumption and energy efficiency, water consumption, food consumption, transport and car choice, waste management and resource efficiency, and compliance with environmental regulation. These chapters make frequent use of the terms defined here.

Which behavioural biases affect environmental policy outcomes?

Behavioural biases are the features of human behaviour that, if observed through the lens of standard economic theory, can be defined as *deviations* from rational decision-making. Following Mullainathan and Thaler (2000), behavioural biases can be grouped into three categories, depending on the behavioural deviation from the characteristics of *homo economicus*: bounded rationality, bounded willower and bounded self-interest. While behavioural sciences have provided evidence for many more behavioural biases, the focus here is on the biases which have the potential to impact environmental policy and its effectiveness.

Bounded rationality

"***Bounded rationality*** reflects the limited cognitive abilities that constrain human problem solving." (Mullainathan and Thaler, 2000)

- ***Framing effect***: the way an option is presented (or framed) affects individual choice among alternatives. More specifically, individuals can draw different conclusions from the same amount of information, depending on how it is presented and the relative salience of its elements.
- ***Loss aversion*** arises when the cost associated with giving up something is perceived as greater than the benefit that would accrue to the acquisition of the same thing (Gsottbauer and van den Bergh, 2011). Loss aversion can help explain the endowment effect and the status-quo bias:
  - ***Endowment effect***: "The value of a good to an individual appears to be higher when the good is viewed as something that could be lost or given up than when the same good is evaluated as a potential gain" (Kahneman, 2003)

- ***Status-quo bias***: "Because the reference point is usually the status quo, the properties of alternative options are evaluated as advantages or disadvantages relative to the current situation, and the disadvantages of the alternatives loom larger than their advantages. This leads to inertia." (Kahneman, 2003)

Bounded willpower

"***Bounded willpower*** captures the fact that people sometimes make choices that are not in their long-run interest." (Mullainathan and Thaler, 2000)

- Inconsistencies between individual beliefs and behaviours can be denoted as ***cognitive dissonances***. This phenomenon leads to an attitude-behaviour gap, a mismatch between beliefs and concrete behaviours. Sometimes, people may react to this mismatch by aligning their beliefs to their behaviour instead of the opposite (Carlsson and Johansson-Stenman, 2012).
- ***Myopia in intertemporal choices***: individuals tend to show time-inconsistent preferences when considering decisions characterised by time-varying discount rates. This means that they will apply discount rates that are higher in the short run than in the long run (hyperbolic discounting), rather than constant over time. In other words, individuals with this type of preferences would rather obtain one Euro today than one Euro tomorrow, but when presented with the choice between receiving one Euro in one year and the same amount in one year and one day, they will gladly wait for an extra day. This type of discounting drives short-sighted decisions, placing disproportionate weight on immediate costs and benefits relatively to long-term ones (Gsottbauer and van den Bergh, 2011).

Bounded self-interest

"***Bounded self-interest*** incorporates the comforting fact that humans are often willing to sacrifice their own interests to help others." (Mullainathan and Thaler, 2000)

- Individuals are not motivated exclusively by their own utility: ***altruism, fairness and social norms*** also affect individual decision-making. While altruism and fairness need not be defined, social norms and their impact on consumer behaviour deserve further scrutiny. People conform to behaviours which are perceived as the norm in society, and compare their own behaviour to these ideal benchmarks.

What are behavioural interventions?

A recent report from the European Commission (Sousa Lourenço et al., 2016) provides a typology of the extent to which behavioural insights have been taken into consideration and have informed the policy process:

- ***Behaviourally tested interventions*** are "initiatives based on an ad-hoc test, or scaled out after an initial experiment";
- ***Behaviourally informed interventions*** are "initiatives designed explicitly on previously existing behavioural evidence"; and
- ***Behaviourally aligned interventions*** are "initiatives that, at least a posteriori, can be found to be aligned to behavioural evidence".

This report focuses solely on behaviourally informed and behaviourally tested interventions, as they are the outcomes of deliberate efforts of policy makers to draw upon behavioural insights when developing and implementing policies. Here, these two types of interventions are denoted as *behavioural interventions*. Conversely, while behaviourally aligned initiatives may be effective in delivering policy results, they are not based on a good understanding of the behavioural mechanisms upon which they act. This limits the possibilities to replicate them in the future or in other contexts.

What types of behavioural levers can policy makers use?

Policy makers can use a range of behavioural levers to design and roll out an appropriate policy intervention. These levers are, in fact, the building blocks of behavioural interventions and, as such, constitute concrete tools for policy makers. Extending the classification provided by Mont, Lehner and Heiskanen (2014), seven main types of ***behavioural levers*** can be distinguished:

- ***Simplification and framing of information***: simplifying complex information can prevent information overload. Framing aims at representing information by consciously activating certain values and attitudes of individuals. The way information is framed can also affect how it is processed by its recipients. For example, energy efficiency labels can be framed to provide a sense of the relative ranking of an electric appliance with respect to the best-in-class one, and the savings that one could enjoy when switching to the latter.
- ***Changes to the physical environment***: the physical environment can substantially affect individual decision-making, especially in contexts in which choices are made spontaneously, on the basis of automated mechanisms and habits. Examples of such interventions are changes in the location and appearance (e.g. colour) of recycling bins, or the installation of automatic (sensor-based) water taps to curb water consumption.
- ***Changes to the default policy***: as individuals are prone to status-quo bias, they often postpone making decisions until or unless it becomes inevitable to do so. Defaults can, thus, have a great impact in contexts in which people are resistant to change. An example of such interventions is a change to the default setting of thermostats (i.e. to a lower baseline temperature in order to foster energy savings).
- ***Use of social norms and comparisons***: as individuals are social beings, not solely driven by their own payoffs, they are affected by the way people surrounding them behave (social norms), by how they compare to their peers (social comparison) as well as by moral injunctions. An example of this type of intervention is the comparison of a household's energy or water consumption to the consumption of a same-sized household in the same neighbourhood.
- ***Use of feedback mechanisms***: several routine behaviours, such as energy consumption or waste disposal, have considerable environmental impacts. However, these impacts are often not sufficiently salient for consumers. Providing them with timely feedback can make such contexts more transparent, increasing awareness of environmental externalities stemming from daily consumption choices. For example, real-time in-home displays connected to smart energy meters can provide real time feedback on energy consumption and costs.
- ***Reward and punishment schemes*** can be used as "carrots and sticks", associating a salient, material payoff to consumers' achievements. For example, rewarding

households who have been particularly savvy with water consumption during scarcity periods may generate a positive norm for water conservation.

- ***Goal setting and commitment devices***: as individuals are bound by status-quo bias and inertia, effortful behaviour changes can be encouraged by setting specific and measurable goals and using commitment devices to regularly follow up on progress. One such example involves pinning down an objective of energy savings and following up on the objective with regular feedback and tips.

Note that "hybrid" interventions can be designed by building upon several of these insights at once. For example, energy conservation can be prompted by reframing energy bills in order to make them more intuitive and by using social comparisons therein.

Price-based policies, instead, leverage the most traditional form of market-based tools, such as taxes, to induce economically rational changes in individual behaviour. They should, thus, not be confused with policies building upon behavioural insights, which aim at tackling behaviours that are not consistent with the model of rational economic behaviour.

What methods can be used to test and assess the impact of behavioural interventions?

Experiments enable the estimation of a policy's causal effect. The cornerstone for credibly identifying the causal effect of a policy is the construction of the correct counterfactual (List and Price, 2016). The idea behind the establishment of a counterfactual is to compare the impact of the policy of interest on a group that is exposed to it (or, in the experimental jargon, "treated" with it), with its impact on a control group, which is unaffected by the policy intervention. The empirical findings of experiments can inform policy makers, motivating the launch of new policies or changes in existing ones.

Harrison and List (2004) argue that ***"[c]ontrolled" experiments***, which include *laboratory experiments* and *field experiments*, represent the most convincing method of creating the counterfactual, since they directly construct a control group via randomization" (p. 1014). In fact, randomisation ensures that the individuals or groups of people exposed to the policy to be tested and those exposed to the control condition are truly comparable (Haynes et al., 2012). Experiments based on the randomised assignment of participants (individuals, households, firms…) to treatment or control groups (in short, randomised treatment allocation) are called ***randomised controlled trials*** or, in short, ***RCTs*** (see also Haynes et al., 2012; Gertler et al., 2016). According to the type of randomisation process, Charness, Gneezy and Kuhn (2012) distinguish two different types of design:

- "In a ***"within-subject" designed experiment***, each individual is exposed to more than one of the treatments being tested, whether it be playing a game with two different parameter values, being treated and untreated, answering multiple questions, or performing tasks under more than one external stimulus. With such designs, as long as there is independence of the multiple exposures, causal estimates can be obtained by examining how individual behavior changed when the circumstances of the experiment changed.

- In a ***"between-subject" designed experiment***, each individual is exposed to only one treatment. With these types of designs, as long as group assignment is random, causal estimates are obtained by comparing the behavior of those in one experimental condition with the behavior of those in another." (Charness, Gneezy and Kuhn, 2012, p. 1)

Likewise, one can talk about *between-group* and *within-group* experimental design, if the randomisation is carried out at the level of *groups* of individuals (e.g. a village, a cohort of students…) rather than at the level of single individuals. According to the experimental context, one can distinguish between:

- ***Laboratory (lab) experiments*** are conducted with volunteer participants in a controlled laboratory facility (Levitt and List, 2009; Noussair and van Soest, 2014).
- ***Field experiments*** are carried out in naturally occurring settings, often with subjects that are unaware of being part of an experiment. Field experiments also include experiments carried out on real online platforms (e.g. e-commerce websites or social networking platforms), which are becoming increasingly popular. Such experiments are denoted in this report by the term ***online field experiments*** (Chen and Konstan, 2015). These should not be confused with experiments carried out on simulated online environments specifically designed for experimental purposes.

How to assess policy impacts when treatment allocation is not randomised? For some of the interventions described in this report, impact evaluation is not based on the randomised assignment of experiment subjects to a treatment or control group. In such cases, causally identifying the impact of the policy intervention requires different methodological approaches based on the analysis of what Levitt and List (2009) call "naturally-occurring data" or "uncontrolled data" (see e.g. Blundell and Costa Dias (2009) for a technical overview of such methods and Gertler et al. (2016) for a non-technical one). This approach to causal identification of policy impacts works as long as the policy is introduced as an "exogenous shock", and randomly – in a statistical sense – allocates subjects to control (unaffected by the policy) and treatment (affected by the policy) groups.

What about stated preference studies? An entirely different category of policy interventions involves stated preference studies, such as ***stated choice experiments***. In this type of experiments, subjects are presented with hypothetical choice scenarios where they have to select their preferred alternative among a menu of hypothetical options (see also Alpízar et al., 2003). This type of experiment can be carried out in the context of a survey (with the help of a questionnaire), or in simulated online environments. The aim of this type of studies is to elicit individual preferences and willingness to pay for specific goods or attributes – usually for those not yet available in the market or those for which no market exists.

References

Alpízar, F., F. Carlsson and P. Martinsson (2003), "Using Choice Experiments for Non-Market Valuation", *Economic Issues*, 8, pp. 83–110.

Blundell, R. and M. Costa Dias (2009), "Alternative approaches to evaluation in empirical microeconomics", *Journal of Human Resources*, 44(3), pp. 565–640, http://dx.doi.org/10.1353/jhr.2009.0009.

Charness, G., U. Gneezy and M. A. Kuhn (2012), "Experimental methods: Between-subject and within-subject design", *Journal of Economic Behavior and Organization*, 81(1), pp. 1–8, http://dx.doi.org/10.1016/j.jebo.2011.08.009.

Chen, Y. and J. Konstan (2015), "Online field experiments: a selective survey of methods", *Journal of the Economic Science Association*, 1(1), pp. 29–42, http://dx.doi.org/10.1007/s40881-015-0005-3.

Gertler, P. J. et al. (2016), *Impact Evaluation in Practice,second edition*, Inter-American Development Bank and World Bank, Washington, DC, http://dx.doi.org/10.1596/978-1-4648-0779-4.

Harrison, G. W. and J. A. List (2004), "Field Experiments", *Journal of Economic Literature*, 42(4), pp. 1009–1055, http://dx.doi.org/10.1257/0022051043004577.

Haynes, L. et al. (2012), *Test, Learn, Adapt: Developing Public Policy with Randomised Controlled Trials*, Cabinet Office Behavioural Insights Team, London.

Kahneman, D. (2003), "Maps of bounded rationality: Psychology for behavioral economics", *The American Economic Review, 93*(5), 1449-1475.

Levitt, S. D. and J. A. List (2009), "Field experiments in economics: The past, the present, and the future", *European Economic Review*, 53(1), pp. 1–18, http://dx.doi.org/10.1016/j.euroecorev.2008.12.001.

List, J. A. and Price, M. K. (2016), "Using Field Experiments in Environmental and Resource Economics", *Review of Environmental Economics and Policy*, 10(2), pp. 206–225, http://dx.doi.org/10.3386/w19289.

Mont, O., Lehner, M. and Heiskanen, E. (2014), *Nudging– A tool for sustainable behaviour?* Swedish Environmental Protection Agency, Stockholm.

Mullainathan, S. and R. Thaler (2000), "Behavioral Economics", *NBER Working Paper Series*, http://www.nber.org/papers/w7948.

Noussair, C. N. and D. P. van Soest (2014), "Economic Experiments and Environmental Policy: A Review", *Annual Review of Resource Economics*, 6(1), pp. 1–27, http://dx.doi.org/10.1146/annurev-resource-091912-151833.

Sousa Lourenço, J. et al. (2016), *Behavioural Insights Applied to Policy. European Report 2016*, Science for Policy report, Joint Research Centre, European Commission, Brussels, http://dx.doi.org/10.2760/903938.

Executive summary

Policy needs to be developed on the basis of realistic representations of the mechanisms driving individual and collective decision-making. Insights from the behavioural sciences, such as behavioural economics, psychology and neuroscience can help policy makers obtain a deeper understanding of the behavioural mechanisms that contribute to environmental problems, and design and implement more effective policy interventions. *Behavioural insights* (BIs) are a complementary tool to traditional policy instruments, such as pricing and regulation.

This report reviews recent developments in the use of BIs in environmentally relevant policy in OECD countries and beyond. It draws on 36 interventions based on behavioural insights, mainly implemented between 2010 and 2016. Focusing on behavioural interventions initiated and/or carried out by government departments and agencies, the report shows what has proven to work – and what has not – in policy practice.

How have governments applied behavioural insights to environmentally relevant policy making?

Governments and institutions have been organising their work on BI applications following two approaches. Some countries have set up in-house behavioural insights teams at a centralised or regional level and/or within the ministry responsible for environmental matters. This approach is followed in Australia, Canada, France, Israel, the Netherlands, South Africa, the United Kingdom and the United States. Other countries have developed *ad-hoc* projects, usually in co-operation with academia or the private sector. This approach is taken by Chile, Colombia, Costa Rica, Denmark, Norway, Sweden, and Switzerland. Germany and the European Commission have adopted both approaches.

Behavioural insights have been applied to a wide array of policy areas: energy, water and food consumption, transport and car choice, waste management and resource efficiency, and compliance with environmental regulation and participation in voluntary schemes.

- ***Encouraging energy conservation and private investment in energy efficiency***: Several governments have used behavioural interventions to promote energy conservation and encourage private investments in more energy efficient technologies. A number of interventions focus on the appropriate framing of energy efficiency labels, with the ultimate goal to increase the uptake of more energy efficient goods. Evidence showing that consumers are sensitive to the way the energy efficiency scale is presented have already been used as input in the European Commission's proposed revision of energy efficiency labels. Furthermore, multiple interventions demonstrate that complementing energy efficiency labels with estimates of lifetime running costs can encourage choosing more efficient household appliances. Other interventions which have been shown to reduce energy consumption include providing real-time feedback on energy consumption through in-home displays, changing default options to more energy-saving settings and benchmarking one's own energy consumption against that of one's peers.

- ***Promoting the purchase of more fuel efficient cars:*** The few BI applications in this domain have investigated the role of alternative fuel efficiency labels and ways of providing information on CO_2 emissions in the purchase of new cars. Evidence shows that complementing labels with information about expected fuel costs over a period of multiple years, and especially benchmarking these costs against those of the most fuel efficient or average car in the same class, can promote the purchase of more fuel efficient models. The US Environmental Protection Agency took this evidence into account when designing their new fuel economy label.
- ***Encouraging water conservation:*** Behavioural interventions to promote water conservation have used a diverse set of levers. Messages on the water bill comparing household's consumption with the average household in the same neighbourhood and guidance on the concrete steps that households can take to save water have been shown to prompt conservation. Likewise, placing stickers emphasising the need to save water next to faucets has also proven to induce conservation. In Switzerland, an interesting intervention showed that using in-home displays to provide real-time feedback on hot water consumption in the shower leads to both energy and water savings.
- ***Incentivising more sustainable food consumption:*** Applications of BIs in this domain have been based on simplifying and framing information about food products. For example, persuasive messages inviting consumers to purchase imperfect-looking food products in order to prevent food waste have been shown to be effective even without substantial price cuts for such products. At the same time, the way in which the optimal quality guarantee of food products is framed (e.g. best-before date vs. production date) determines consumers' perceptions of their quality and safety and eventually whether consumers will throw away groceries while they are still perfectly safe for consumption. These insights have already motivated the European Commission to consider simplifying date markings on food products.
- ***Preventing waste and encourage resource efficiency:*** Governments have used behavioural interventions to prevent the disposal of electronic devices, incentivise the purchase of durable goods with a longer lifespan, reduce (printer) paper use in government offices and decrease littering. Behavioural levers for these purposes include changing default settings, using social comparisons, and framing information in more understandable ways. For instance, evidence from the Netherlands shows that littering in the immediate surroundings of waste containers can be significantly reduced if containers are tagged with stickers informing individuals that most people in their neighbourhood do not litter. Littering can also be prevented by reminding individuals that it results in a fine.
- ***Promoting environmental compliance and participation in voluntary schemes:*** Behavioural insights can also help increase the compliance of firms and individuals with environmental regulation as well as the participation of firms in voluntary schemes. Behavioural interventions used for this purpose range from clearly framing relevant pieces of information to make them more salient, and to sending regulated entities reminders of their obligations at key moments, to priming messages underlining the environmental benefits and competitive advantages associated with voluntary environmental certification. For example, messages emphasising the mandatory nature of these obligations, combined with timely reminders, were

shown to increase firms' compliance with reporting requirements by the Australian Department of the Environment. Messages highlighting the consequences of not complying have also proven to be effective.

Cross-cutting challenges and opportunities for future applications of behavioural insights

While the different policy areas covered in this report differ in the potential that BI applications hold for them, some key challenges are cross-cutting across domains. One such challenge is generalisability: the extent to which findings from a behavioural intervention implemented in a specific (geographical, cultural and behavioural) context can be transferred to a different one is questionable. Another major issue for behavioural interventions is that little is known about the persistence of their effects over time.

Opportunities are instead apparent in cross-fertilisation across different policy areas characterised by similar behavioural biases. For example, both water and energy conservation can be incentivised through interventions based on social comparisons and interventions providing real-time feedback on consumption. At the same time, because behavioural sciences are strongly rooted in rigorous empirical assessment, BIs can contribute to mainstreaming a culture of evidence-based environmental policy making. This translates into learning from behavioural interventions and consequently adapting policies based on what has been empirically proven to work. Empirical evidence of policy outcomes can, in all contexts, help deliver better policies.

Many governments have made significant efforts to use insights from behavioural sciences to tackle environmental problems. While evidence of the potential contribution of BI applications to energy-related objectives exists, more efforts are needed to pinpoint how other policy areas can benefit from unlocking the untapped potential of BIs. Promising domains for the application of BIs include waste management and resource efficiency, transport, water, and environmental compliance.

Chapter 1

How can behavioural insights help tackle environmental problems?

Behavioural biases can affect the outcomes of policies aiming to tackle environmental problems. This chapter provides examples of such behavioural biases and explains how behavioural insights can inform policy making in this realm. It provides a typology of behavioural levers that can act as complements for traditional environmental policy tools. It then synthesises the main lessons learnt from behavioural interventions implemented by governments in a range of policy areas: energy, water and food consumption, transport and car choice, waste management and resource efficiency, compliance with environmental regulation and participation in voluntary schemes. It concludes with an overview of the cross-cutting issues in the application of behavioural insights to environmentally relevant policy, and proposes directions for future applications.

The statistical data for Israel are supplied by and under the responsibility of the relevant Israeli authorities. The use of such data by the OECD is without prejudice to the status of the Golan Heights, East Jerusalem and Israeli settlements in the West Bank under the terms of international law.

Individual and collective decision-making, from daily consumption decisions to once-in-a-lifetime investments, can give rise to or worsen environmental problems. The outcome of relevant policies depends on whether they can provide individuals, households, organisations and firms with incentives to make more environmentally sustainable decisions. Hence, policies need to be developed on the basis of realistic representations of the mechanisms driving individual and collective decision-making. Individuals do not always behave in a self-interested way, optimising their actions under perfect self-control, as postulated in standard economic theory. On the contrary, individual decision-making is constrained by limited cognitive resources and bounded willpower (see Box 1.1), and it is often influenced by consideration of other people's well-being: this is ultimately reflected in consumption and investment decisions, as well as in decisions regarding compliance with environmental regulation.

Insights from behavioural sciences – *behavioural insights* or *BIs* – can help policy makers obtain a deeper understanding of the behavioural mechanisms contributing to environmentally harmful choices and develop more effective policies to address environmental problems. Behavioural insights can be used both to improve the effectiveness of existing policy instruments and to devise new ones, providing another arrow in policy makers' quiver to prompt more environmentally sustainable behaviours. They should not be viewed as a substitute, but as a complementary – and, in most cases, low-cost – tool to traditional environmental policy instruments, such as pricing and regulation.

This report reviews recent developments in the application of behavioural insights to the diagnosis of the causes of environmental problems and to the design, implementation and evaluation of environmentally relevant policy in OECD countries and beyond. A variety of policy areas are covered: energy, water and food consumption, transport and car choice, waste management and resource efficiency, compliance with environmental regulation and participation in voluntary schemes. By focusing on a limited range of environmentally relevant policy areas, it is possible both to delve deeper into the behavioural biases pertinent to each of them, and to provide a more detailed description of applications, zooming on design choices and their empirical results. At the same time, the OECD is also working on applications of behavioural insights to a broader set of policy domains, from regulatory to consumer policy (OECD, 2017a; 2017b).

The report's focus is on applications initiated and/or carried out by governmental entities such as ministries, environment agencies and specialised behavioural insights teams. Applications initiated by the private sector, research institutions or the academia are, thus, not reviewed; for reviews of such applications, see e.g. Carlsson and Johansson-Stenman (2012), Gsottbauer and van den Bergh (2011) and Shogren (2012).

The report analyses 36 applications of behavioural insights, mainly implemented between 2010 and 2016. Information on these interventions has been gathered from published reports and direct communications with the teams in charge of their design and implementation. While the report has no ambition to provide an exhaustive overview of all the policy-making endeavours building upon behavioural sciences, it offers a snapshot of the insights that have thus far been tested and used in environmentally relevant policy making. By synthesising evidence from various countries, this work facilitates the exchange of results and best practices.

What can policy makers learn from behavioural sciences?

The reason why behavioural sciences, and more specifically behavioural economics, are increasingly informing policy making in a range of policy areas is that standard economic theory does not always provide a realistic framework to understand and predict individual behaviour (Kahneman and Tversky, 1979; Simon, 1955, 1959; Thaler, 1980; Tversky and Kahneman, 1981). This theoretical framework postulates that all individuals make decisions – be they on a daily basis, such as food consumption choices, or on a more infrequent one, such as the purchase of a car – based on the same utility maximisation exercise and with complete information. Individuals act under perfect self-control and considering nothing but their own self-interest. Moreover, they have well-formed and time-consistent preferences, which remain unaffected by the way the decision is framed or by the impact it has on others (DellaVigna, 2009). This type of decision-maker is often denoted as *homo economicus.*

Homo economicus's decision-making process does not always match observed individual behaviour, which is affected by a complex set of drivers ranging from cognitive limitations to emotions. Individual decision-making is often dependent on framing and reference points, altruism, and heuristic methods (Kahneman et al., 1986; Tversky and Kahneman, 1974, 1981). Through the standard economic lens, these features of human behaviour can be seen as *deviations* from rational decision-making: for this reason, in economic literature they are often labelled as behavioural *biases* or *limitations.*

Following Mullainathan and Thaler (2000), such behavioural biases can be grouped into three categories, depending on the behavioural deviation from the characteristics of *homo economicus*: "*Bounded rationality* reflects the limited cognitive abilities that constrain human problem solving. *Bounded willpower* captures the fact that people sometimes make choices that are not in their long-run interest. *Bounded self-interest* incorporates the comforting fact that humans are often willing to sacrifice their own interests to help others." Box 1.1 describes the behavioural biases which have the potential to impact environmental policy and its effectiveness, grouping them in these three categories. These definitions, used extensively throughout the report, are also provided in the reader's guide for convenience.

Box 1.1. Behavioural biases impacting environmental policy

While behavioural sciences have provided evidence for many more behavioural biases, the focus here is on the biases which have the potential to impact environmental policy and its effectiveness. For extensive reviews of behavioural biases, see DellaVigna (2009) and Kahneman (2003).

Bounded rationality

Framing effect: the way an option is presented (or framed) affects individual choice among alternatives. More specifically, individuals can draw different conclusions from the same amount of information, depending on how it is presented and on the relative salience of its elements.

Loss aversion arises when the cost associated with giving up something is perceived as greater than the benefit that would accrue to the acquisition of the same thing (Gsottbauer and van den Bergh, 2011). Loss aversion can help explain the endowment effect and the status-quo bias. In Kahneman's (2003) words:

Endowment effect: "The value of a good to an individual appears to be higher when the good is viewed as something that could be lost or given up than when the same good is evaluated as a potential gain".

Box 1.1. **Behavioural biases impacting environmental policy** *(continued)*

Status-quo bias: "Because the reference point is usually the status quo, the properties of alternative options are evaluated as advantages or disadvantages relative to the current situation, and the disadvantages of the alternatives loom larger than their advantages. This leads to inertia."

Bounded willpower

Inconsistencies between individual beliefs and behaviours can be denoted as *cognitive dissonances*. This phenomenon leads to an attitude-behaviour gap, a mismatch between beliefs and concrete behaviours. Sometimes, people may react to this mismatch by aligning their beliefs to their behaviour instead of the opposite (Carlsson and Johansson-Stenman, 2012).

Myopia in intertemporal choices: individuals tend to show time-inconsistent preferences when considering decisions characterised by time-varying discount rates. This means that they will apply discount rates that are higher in the short run than in the long run (hyperbolic discounting), rather than constant over time. In other words, individuals with this type of preferences would rather obtain one Euro today than one Euro tomorrow, but when presented with the choice between receiving one Euro in one year and the same amount in one year and one day, they will gladly wait for an extra day. This type of discounting drives short-sighted decisions, placing disproportionate weight on immediate costs and benefits relatively to long-term ones (Gsottbauer and van den Bergh, 2011).

Bounded self-interest

Individuals are not motivated exclusively by their own utility: *altruism, fairness and social norms* also affect individual decision-making. While altruism and fairness need not be defined, social norms and their impact on consumer behaviour deserve further scrutiny. People conform to behaviours which are perceived as the norm in society, and compare their own behaviour to these ideal benchmarks.

Sources: Carlsson and Johansson-Stenman (2012); DellaVigna (2009); Gsottbauer and van den Bergh (2011); Kahneman (2003).

Behavioural economics is a field of economics that, borrowing insights from psychology, seeks to identify the ways in which human behaviour deviates from the standard economic model and to show how these behavioural biases matter in an economic context (Mullainathan and Thaler, 2000). This field of research is only one of the branches of *behavioural sciences*, which also include cognitive and social psychology, sociology and neurosciences (Sousa Lourenço et al., 2016). Building on a diverse range of research methods, these disciplines analyse the mechanisms driving human behaviour. Taking stock of recent advances in behavioural economics and, more broadly, behavioural sciences, can enable the design of more economically efficient and environmentally effective policy interventions (OECD, 2015).

What are behavioural interventions and what are their roles in policy making?

A recent report from the European Commission (Sousa Lourenço et al., 2016) provides a typology of policy interventions developed by taking into consideration behavioural insights. *Behaviourally tested interventions* are defined as "initiatives based on an ad-hoc test, or scaled out after an initial experiment"; *behaviourally informed interventions* as "initiatives designed explicitly on previously existing behavioural evidence"; and *behaviourally aligned interventions* as "initiatives that, at least a posteriori, can be found to be aligned to behavioural evidence".

The present report focuses solely on behaviourally informed and behaviourally tested interventions, as they are the outcomes of deliberate efforts of policy makers to draw upon behavioural insights when developing and implementing policies. Here, these two types of interventions are denoted as *behavioural interventions*. Conversely, while behaviourally aligned initiatives may be effective in delivering policy results, they are not based on a good understanding of the behavioural mechanisms upon which they act. This limits the possibilities to replicate them in the future or in other contexts.

When it comes to their role in the policy making process, behavioural insights can be thought of as tools with a triple use:

1. *Problem diagnosis*: policy makers can exploit behavioural insights to recognise the behavioural patterns and diagnose the behavioural biases contributing to the environmental problem they aim to tackle. This is necessary for the identification of the behavioural levers on which effective policy interventions should rely. A deeper understanding of the cognitive mechanisms at the core of individual decision-making can pave the way for more effective design, implementation and evaluation of policies to tackle environmentally damaging behaviours.
2. *Policy design and implementation*: once a given behavioural bias has been identified as causing environmental damage, behavioural insights can inform the design and implementation of policies, building upon a more realistic view of individual behaviour and its interaction with environmental policy instruments. Policy makers can use a range of behavioural levers to design and roll out an appropriate policy intervention. Extending the classification provided by by Mont, Lehner and Heiskanen (2014), seven main types of behavioural levers can be distinguished. These levers are, in fact, the building blocks of behavioural interventions and, as such, constitute concrete tools for policy makers: they are described in detail in Box 1.2. These definitions, used extensively throughout the report, are also provided in the reader's guide for convenience.
3. *Policy evaluation*: applying behavioural insights to policy making motivates a thorough evaluation approach. In order to test the effectiveness of a certain behavioural intervention, its outcomes should be empirically assessed. Measurable indicators of policy effectiveness should be defined *prior* to implementing the intervention. Analysing variations in these indicators allows evaluating whether the intervention has been successful according to policy makers' objectives.

Box 1.2. **Typology of behavioural levers**

The following typology of behavioural levers builds upon the one proposed by Mont, Lehner and Heiskanen (2014).

- *Simplification and framing of information*: simplifying complex information can prevent information overload. Framing aims at representing information by consciously activating certain values and attitudes of individuals. The way information is framed can also affect how it is processed by its recipients. For example, energy efficiency labels can be framed to provide a sense of the relative ranking of an electric appliance with respect to the best-in-class one, and the savings that one could enjoy when switching to the latter.

Box 1.2. **Typology of behavioural levers** *(continued)*

- *Changes to the physical environment*: the physical environment can substantially affect individual decision-making, especially in contexts in which choices are made spontaneously, on the basis of automated mechanisms and habits. Examples of such interventions are changes in the location and appearance (e.g. colour) of recycling bins, or the installation of automatic (sensor-based) water taps to curb water consumption.
- *Changes to the default policy*: as individuals are prone to status-quo bias, they often postpone making decisions until or unless it becomes inevitable to do so. Defaults can, thus, have a great impact in contexts in which people are resistant to change. An example of such interventions is a change to the default setting of thermostats (i.e. to a lower baseline temperature in order to foster energy savings).
- *Use of social norms and comparisons*: as individuals are social beings, not solely driven by their own payoffs, they are affected by the way people surrounding them behave (social norms), by how they compare to their peers (social comparison) as well as by moral injunctions. An example of this type of intervention is the comparison of a household's energy or water consumption to the consumption of a same-sized household in the same neighbourhood.
- *Use of feedback mechanisms*: several routine behaviours, such as energy consumption or waste disposal, have considerable environmental impacts. However, these impacts are often not sufficiently salient for consumers. Providing them with timely feedback can make such contexts more transparent, increasing awareness of environmental externalities stemming from daily consumption choices. For example, real-time in-home displays connected to smart energy meters can provide real time feedback on energy consumption and costs.
- *Reward and punishment schemes* can be used as "carrots and sticks", associating a salient, material payoff to consumers' achievements. For example, rewarding households who have been particularly savvy with water consumption during scarcity periods may generate a positive norm for water conservation.
- *Goal setting and commitment devices*: as individuals are bound by status-quo bias and inertia, effortful behaviour changes can be encouraged by setting specific and measurable goals and using commitment devices to regularly follow up on progress. One such example involves pinning down an objective of energy savings and following up on the objective with regular feedback and tips.

Note that "hybrid" interventions can be designed by building upon several of these insights at once. For example, energy conservation can be prompted by reframing energy bills in order to make them more intuitive and by using social comparisons therein.

Price-based policies, instead, leverage the most traditional form of market-based tools, such as taxes, to induce economically rational changes in individual behaviour. They should, thus, not be confused with behaviourally motivated policies, which aim at tackling behaviours that are not consistent with the model of rational economic behaviour.

Source: adapted and extended from Mont, Lehner and Heiskanen (2014).

The application of quantitative and qualitative methods is at the core of *evidence-based policy making.* Quantitative methods (e.g. experiments) are necessary for obtaining an empirical assessment of the impact of policy interventions, which can be complemented by rich insights from qualitative analysis (e.g. interviews). This translates into designing and launching policy pilots based on behavioural insights, learning from their results and consequently adapting policies on the basis of what has been empirically proven to work. The London-based Behavioural Insights Team has summarised this approach with the motto "test, learn, adapt" (Haynes et al., 2012). Behavioural interventions are increasingly associated with rigorous empirical evaluation of their impacts. However, this approach could very well also apply to the implementation of traditional environmental policy tools. Empirical evidence of policy outcomes can, in all contexts, help assess policy effectiveness and deliver better policies.

What do we know? Overview of policy experiences and lessons learned

Governments and institutions at different territorial levels have been organising their work on applications of behavioural insights to tackle environmental problems following two main approaches. The first approach is to set up in-house behavioural insights teams at a centralised or regional level, or within the ministry or agency responsible for environmental issues. The second approach is to develop ad-hoc projects, usually in co-operation with academia or the private sector. Chapter 2 further explores the differences in governance, scope and methodology that have so far characterised behavioural interventions in environmental policy making.

Behavioural interventions tackling environmental problems have pursued a broad range of objectives: i) encourage conservation of resources, such as energy, water and materials; ii) promote private investment in more efficient technologies; iii) incentivise environmentally sustainable consumption patterns; and iv) increase compliance with environmental regulation and participation in voluntary schemes, both on the side of individuals and firms. Next, the main lessons from the report are synthetically presented by policy objective, referring both to the behavioural biases under scrutiny and the behavioural levers on which policy interventions are built. Technical terms are defined in the reader's guide.

Encourage resource conservation

Residential energy and water conservation are frequently hampered by poor communication of real-time information on consumption levels and associated costs to end-users. For example, households rarely know how much electricity is consumed when baking a meal in an electric oven or using the washing machine. Likewise, they are usually ignorant about the amount of water consumed when taking a shower or washing the dishes.

Pairing smart meters with visible devices that provide *real-time feedback* to consumers, such as real-time in-home displays and smartphone apps, increases the salience of information on consumption and has been effective in promoting resource conservation (at least in the energy domain). Levers based on *social comparisons*, such as benchmarking household consumption against that of relevant social groups (e.g. same-size households in the same neighbourhood), can also help conserve energy and water.

Framing information about resource consumption and costs – especially in utility bills – in a simpler and more salient way can also contribute to conservation efforts. Resource conservation can also be encouraged through *changes in the physical environment*, such as the installation of intuitively designed thermostats or the placement of stickers encouraging savings next to water taps. *Greening default settings*, such as switching from one-sided to double-sided printing, can also help save valuable resources.

It is worth noting that a careful coupling of two or more of the aforementioned interventions may enhance their effectiveness (e.g. simultaneously providing real-time feedback and information about how a household's consumption compares with the consumption of comparable households). Similar interventions to the ones described above can also promote energy conservation in office environments, e.g. using inter-office competitions to leverage social comparisons.

Promote private investment in more efficient technologies

Bounded willpower is often responsible for individuals' failure to make investments which are in their long-term interest, such as certain investments in more efficient technologies. Efficiency labels (e.g. energy or fuel efficiency labels) can play an important role in directing consumers to purchases of more efficient products. However, the *framing* of efficiency labels is a crucial driver of their effectiveness in promoting such investments. Framing products' efficiency labels in a more salient and intuitive way and ensuring that they are visible at all decision making stages, are effective ways of stimulating the purchase of more efficient products.

Enriching labels with salient information on the long-run monetary savings from the use of more efficient products – both in absolute terms and in comparison with the best product in class – helps consumers weigh out the costs and benefits of investing in efficiency. This has proven to work for high consumption products (e.g. cars, washer-dryers), but further testing is needed to assess whether this is also the case with lower consumption ones.

Incentivise environmentally sustainable consumption patterns

Individuals often have difficulties in understanding information about the environmental impact of certain products. Information about CO_2 emissions, for example, is not directly translated to specific environmental impacts and individuals rarely have an understanding of differences in the environmental impact between local produce and goods produced thousands of kilometres away.

Framing product information (e.g. labels, in-store banners) in a simpler way to encourage more environmentally sustainable consumption patterns is a promising application of behavioural insights. For example, persuasive messages inviting consumers to purchase imperfect-looking food products in order to prevent food waste have been shown to be effective even without substantial price cuts for such products relative to their perfect-looking counterparts. At the same time, information about the environmental footprint of consumer goods, as well as indicators of CO_2 emissions and air pollution from new cars, deserve a more thorough explanation to provide an actual grip on purchase decisions.

Increase environmental compliance and participation in voluntary schemes

Individuals may not always comply with environmental regulation, because they may find it too complex or unclear, or simply because they believe that the regulation is not strictly enforced. Littering is one of the best examples of individuals' non-compliance, in this case to regulation governing waste disposal. Behavioural levers that have been shown to help reduce littering include *changes in the physical environment*, such as placing signs inviting households to keep the neighbourhood clean. These changes can be more effective if signs also leverage *social comparisons*, by e.g. informing potential offenders that the majority of their peers comply with the regulation. *Framing* signs in such a way that emphasis is placed on the consequences of non-compliance (e.g. size of the corresponding fine) is also an effective strategy to increase compliance, leveraging loss aversion.

While behavioural insights can help policy makers gain a better understanding of individual behaviour, they can also help them understand and influence the behaviour of firms. Employees responsible for e.g. ensuring compliance with environmental standards may also be subject to standard behavioural biases. For example, bounded rationality may prevent their full understanding of complex regulatory requirements or let them underestimate the probability that their firm is closely monitored. Inertia may prevent firms from participating in voluntary schemes (e.g. carbon neutral certification) which may bring along competitive advantages together with environmental benefits.

Simplifying communications from overseeing authorities (e.g. environment agencies) to overseen entities (e.g. small and medium enterprises, but also individuals) has already proved to deliver higher compliance. Simplification ranges from clearly *framing* the pieces of information that matter to make them more salient, to sending reminders of mandatory obligations at key moments. Emphasising the mandatory nature of these obligations and highlighting the consequences of non-compliance has also been shown to promote environmental compliance.

What do we still need to address? Cross-cutting issues

As behavioural insights gain recognition as a tool to identify needs for policy action and increase policy effectiveness, research efforts should be directed towards a number of cross-cutting issues regarding their application. Important cross-cutting issues in this context are the evaluation of the time-persistence and transferability of the effects driven by behavioural interventions, and the assessment of how such interventions can interact with more traditional policy instruments.

Assessing the time-persistence and transferability of identified effects

A key cross-cutting issue that deserves to be further researched is whether and to what extent findings from behavioural interventions run in a specific (geographical, cultural and behavioural) context can be readily transferred to a completely different one. When analysing results from behaviourally tested interventions, it is important to bear in mind that they are related to interventions designed and rolled out for a specific policy context. While such results provide useful insights for policy makers across the OECD and beyond, they should be tested in different policy and geographical contexts.

Piloting the same behavioural intervention in multiple contexts (e.g. in different countries) would allow disentangling the impact of the intervention from context-specific noise. Furthermore, piloting a behavioural intervention on heterogeneous subgroups of the population of interest allows the empirical assessment of possible variations in its impact across groups. This can inform policy-makers about the extent to which specific policy interventions need to be tailored to deal with subgroups' specificities.

Another major issue for behaviourally motivated policies is that little is known about the *persistence* of their effects *over time*. Pushing forward the horizon of pilot testing and related data collection is necessary in order to understand whether and to what extent a behavioural intervention generates persistent results.

Combining behavioural interventions with other policy instruments

Few research efforts have, thus far, been devoted to the ways in which behavioural interventions can interact with other policy instruments. Much of existing research has focused on the complementarity between regulatory instruments and BI interventions. Nevertheless, behavioural insights can also reinforce the impact of market-based instruments, such as pricing. Behavioural biases like loss aversion and myopia are also at play when individuals consider current and future prices, so behavioural levers have a role to play in ensuring that these prices are salient when individuals make investment and consumption decisions.

What's next? Proposals for future applications of behavioural insights

This report demonstrates that a number of governments have made significant efforts to incorporate insights from behavioural sciences in environmentally relevant policy making. However, policy makers can still noticeably improve the effectiveness of policies by unlocking the untapped potential of behavioural insights, especially in the domains of waste management and resource efficiency, transport, water, and environmental compliance. In unlocking this potential, policy makers can both draw on successful applications of BIs in related domains (e.g. apply insights which have proven to promote fuel efficiency investments to policy aiming to encourage the adoption of energy efficient household appliances) and on novel applications.

Test successful applications of behavioural insights in other policy areas and contexts

Applications of behavioural insights to environmentally relevant policy have, thus far, mostly focused on the energy domain (energy conservation, energy efficiency). As water consumption is prone to the same behavioural biases as energy consumption, the low hanging fruit is to test the performance of behavioural interventions that have proven to be successful in the energy domain in the water policy context. This also includes testing promising interventions which draw on multiple behavioural levers, such as combining real-time feedback with the use of social comparisons.

Another straightforward extension is testing in an office environment those behavioural interventions which have proved to work in dwellings. While much attention has been paid to programmes aiming to encourage households to conserve resources (e.g. energy and water) at home, less emphasis has been placed on resource conservation in office environments. *Changes to the physical environment* (e.g. user-friendly thermostat design, motion detector lighting, automatic sensor taps) and *default settings* (e.g. lower baseline heating temperatures) in offices are only a couple of examples of the behavioural levers on which future interventions can draw. Government buildings and offices provide an interesting and often convenient setting for the testing of such interventions.

Design and implement novel applications of behavioural insights

In the energy domain, BIs could also play an important role in providing households with incentives to adopt *"green" electricity contracts*. The behavioural factors explaining low uptake of "green" electricity contracts could be e.g. low awareness of such options, administrative or physical barriers to enrolment, and information/choice overload. *Green default options* are worth considering, by e.g. providing default contracts with a higher share of renewable energy or asking consumers to actively choose the share of renewables in the energy mix offered by their contract. Increasing the salience of the energy mix on which electricity contracts are based could also incentivise consumers to shift to the contract with the energy mix best matching their preferences. More generally, enhancing the transparency of energy bills (e.g. on the costs of electricity consumption and the energy mix used) may help improve the effectiveness of policies in this domain.

Behavioural insights could also help individuals make more environmentally *sustainable vehicle choices.* Individuals often have a hard time understanding indicators of vehicles' CO_2 emissions and environmental performance and associating them with concrete environmental outcomes. Making *changes in the physical environment* (e.g. using stickers to clearly indicate emissions of different pollutants) and *framing* information about environmental performance in a way that reveals transparently and more clearly the environmental and health effects associated with car use are behavioural interventions deserving further consideration.

Behavioural sciences could also inform *urban planning policies*, e.g. when it comes to implementing *changes to the physical environment* such as the design and positioning of cycle paths or the distribution of car and bike parking spots. *Nature conservation* efforts could also be supported by the applications of behavioural insights. One such application could deal with *social-comparison*-based interventions to prevent forest wildfires.

Environmental footprint or sustainability information carries a complex meaning that is hard for consumers to process when having to juggle several other criteria (e.g. price, nutritional value). This deserves more attention, notably in terms of product and label design, and by testing new applications in a context that is familiar to consumers. Such behavioural applications may, for example, exploit different ways of *framing* information about the environmental footprint of different consumer products or the use of persuasive messages promoting a more prudent consumption of high-environmental-impact ones. Such interventions could also be used to decrease consumption of food with particularly negative environmental impact, such as red meat.

Changes to the physical environment could play an important role in increasing rates of waste separation at source and recycling (at home or at collection points). Possible such interventions that deserve testing include: i) the provision of sorting bins to separate waste at home (such bins should be designed to make sorting as intuitive and automatic as possible); ii) the provision of paper or online maps of recycling facilities to households; iii) the concentration of outdoor bins in a single location to simplify and centralise sorting; and iv) the implementation of door-to-door collection of waste instead of sorting at recycling centres, in order to ease the sorting process and make sorting efforts more visible to neighbours, possibly leveraging social comparisons. It is worth mentioning that some of these interventions entail relatively high costs. This is perhaps one of the main reasons for the limited application of changes to physical environment in this area. Indicators for tracking the evolution of e.g. waste generation or recycling are not as easy to design. Furthermore, monitoring progress achieved by such interventions would require specific infrastructure or in-person checks – both rather costly solutions.

Possible lower-cost interventions to increase recycling rates include enhancing the salience of environmental externalities due to waste generation and leveraging *social comparisons.* At the same time, *waste generation* could be reduced by designing incentive schemes prompting consumers to opt for e.g. packaging-free products, whenever possible.

Applications of behavioural insights have largely focused on understanding and influencing individual behaviour. There is still ample scope for investigating the potential of such applications in understanding and influencing the *behaviour of firms.* For example, the uptake of voluntary measures (e.g. Energy Star certification schemes; carbon neutral recognition) by businesses could be increased by making more salient the positive impact they can have on firms' business profile. Behavioural interventions may be especially useful when it comes to changing the behaviour of small enterprises, where decision-making often suffers from the same behavioural biases as individual decision-making.

Behavioural interventions inducing changes to within-firm approaches to environmental problems can also be particularly effective. For example, top management encouragement to engage in more sustainable commuting or consumption patterns may have a strong influence on employees' behaviour. Policy can stimulate such changes by, for example, organising inter-firm competitions on environmental performance and publically rewarding winners and penalising heavy polluters.

References

Carlsson, F. and O. Johansson-Stenman (2012), "Behavioral Economics and Environmental Policy", *Annual Review of Resource Economics*, 4(1), pp. 75–99, http://dx.doi.org/10.1146/annurev-resource-110811-114547.

DellaVigna, S. (2009), "Psychology and economics: evidence from the field", *Journal of Economic Literature*, 47(2), pp. 315–37, http://dx.doi.org/10.1257/jel.47.2.315.

Gsottbauer, E. and J. C. J. M. van den Bergh (2011), "Environmental Policy Theory Given Bounded Rationality and Other-regarding Preferences", *Environmental and Resource Economics*, 49(2), pp. 263–304, http://dx.doi.org/10.1007/s10640-010-9433-y.

Haynes, L. et al. (2012), *Test, Learn, Adapt: Developing Public Policy with Randomised Controlled Trials*, Cabinet Office Behavioural Insights Team, London.

Kahneman, D. (2003), "Maps of bounded rationality: Psychology for behavioral economics", *The American Economic Review, 93*(5), 1449-1475.

Kahneman, D., J. L. Knetsch and R. Thaler (1986), "Fairness as a constraint on profit seeking: Entitlements in the market", *The American Economic Review*, 76(4), pp. 728–741.

Kahneman, D. and A. Tversky (1979), "Prospect Theory: An Analysis of Decision under Risk", *Econometrica*, 47(2), pp. 263–292, http://dx.doi.org/10.2307/1914185.

Mont, O., Lehner, M. and Heiskanen, E. (2014), *Nudging – A tool for sustainable behaviour?* Swedish Environmental Protection Agency, Stockholm.

Mullainathan, S. and R. Thaler (2000), "Behavioral Economics", *NBER Working Paper Series*, http://www.nber.org/papers/w7948.

OECD (2017a), "Use of Behavioural Insights in Consumer Policy", *OECD Science, Technology and Industry Policy Papers*, No. 36, OECD Publishing, Paris, http://dx.doi.org/10.1787/c2203c35-en.

OECD (2017b), *Behavioural Insights and Public Policy: Lessons from Around the World*, OECD Publishing, Paris, http://dx.doi.org/10.1787/9789264270480-en.

OECD (2015), *Final NAEC Synthesis. New Approaches to Economic Challenges*, report for the Meeting of the OECD Council at Ministerial Level, June 2015, OECD, Paris, www.oecd.org/mcm/documents/Final-NAEC-Synthesis-Report-CMIN2015-2.pdf.

Simon, H. A. (1955), "A Behavioral Model of Rational Choice", *The Quarterly Journal of Economics*, 69(1), pp. 99–118.

Simon, H. A. (1959), "Theories of Decision-Making in Economics and Behavioral Science", *The American Economic Review*, 49(3), pp. 253–283.

Sousa Lourenço, J. et al. (2016), *Behavioural Insights Applied to Policy. European Report 2016*, Science for Policy report, Joint Research Centre, European Commission, Brussels, http://dx.doi.org/10.2760/903938.

Thaler, R. (1980), "Toward a positive theory of consumer choice", *Journal of Economic Behavior & Organization*, 1(1), pp. 39–60, http://dx.doi.org/10.1016/0167-2681(80)90051-7.

Tversky, A. and D. Kahneman (1981), "The framing of decisions and the psychology of choice.", *Science*, 211, pp. 453–458, http://dx.doi.org/10.1126/science.7455683.

Tversky, A. and D. Kahneman (1974), "Judgment under Uncertainty: Heuristics and Biases", *Science*, 185, pp. 1124–1131, http://dx.doi.org/10.1126/science.185.4157.1124.

Chapter 2

Mapping out applications of behavioural insights to environmentally relevant policy

This chapter provides a snapshot of the governance approaches that different governments have adopted in leveraging behavioural insights to tackle environmental problems. It maps out the policy areas where behavioural interventions have been developed, and specifies the behavioural levers that policy makers have used to design them. Finally, it outlines the most common methodologies applied in assessing the impacts of behavioural interventions.

The statistical data for Israel are supplied by and under the responsibility of the relevant Israeli authorities. The use of such data by the OECD is without prejudice to the status of the Golan Heights, East Jerusalem and Israeli settlements in the West Bank under the terms of international law.

Governance

Different governance levels may be better positioned to apply behavioural insights to tackle different environmental problems. Certification schemes for fuel efficiency and energy efficiency, for instance, have been tested at the national, federal or international (e.g. European Union) level to support the adoption of more efficient products. On the other hand, interventions acting upon services provided at municipal level (e.g. local transport, water supply, waste collection management) can be launched and monitored more easily at that level. These factors are reflected in the increasingly active role that different administrative levels have been taking up in applications of behavioural insights: from teams and projects launched within city administrations, to teams within a prime minister's office, to specialised units within a given ministry or government agency.

Since the launch of the pioneering Behavioural Insights Team in the United Kingdom in 2010, governments and institutions at different territorial levels have been organising their work on applications of behavioural insights to environmentally relevant policy following two main approaches:

1. Setting up in-house *behavioural insights teams*:
    a. at centralised or regional level, working on a range of policy areas (Australia, Canada, European Commission, France, Germany, United Kingdom, United States and South Africa),
    b. within the Ministry of Environment, working specifically on environmental policy (Australia, Israel, The Netherlands).
2. Developing *ad-hoc projects,* usually in co-operation with consulting firms, NGOs, international organisations or universities or research centres specialised in the development of behavioural interventions and the assessment of their impacts (Chile, Colombia, Costa Rica, Denmark, European Commission, the European Economic and Social Committee, Germany, the Nordic Council, Norway, Sweden, Switzerland).[1]

Within both groups, there is substantial heterogeneity in the extent to which countries and institutions have embraced the integration of behavioural insights in policy making. This translates in different levels of financial and human resources devoted to this process. In general, countries and institutions which have chosen to build an internal specialised team currently seem to be more advanced than their counterparts which have started to explore the potential of behavioural interventions solely through external partnerships. This is apparent both in the scope of the interventions that have been implemented (i.e. the range of policy areas covered) and in the sophistication of methodologies applied in this process. The next sections discuss these two points.

Scope

This report analyses 36 behavioural interventions, mainly implemented between 2010 and 2016. As shown in Figure 2.1, the vast majority of interventions developed so far have focused on energy consumption and energy efficiency investments (18 applications). This is due to the importance of energy policy in the context of climate change action, and to the fact that monitoring energy consumption is relatively easy and, thus, facilitates empirical impact assessment (see chapter 3).

Figure 2.1. **Scope of reviewed BI applications to environmentally relevant policy**

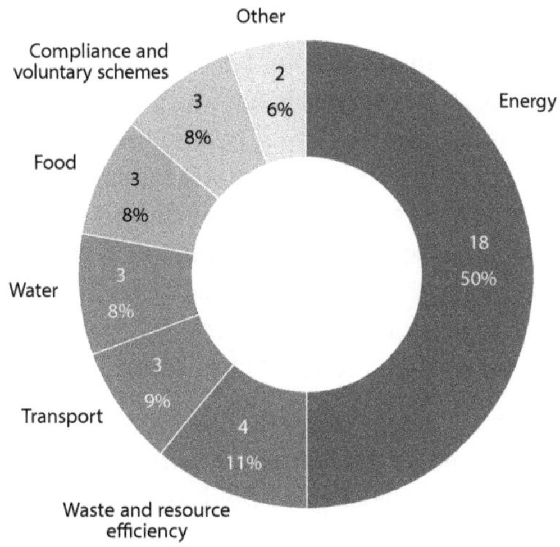

Note: The labels indicate the number of BI applications belonging to each policy domain, and their percentage with respect to the total number of BI applications analysed in this report (36).

Interventions developed in other policy areas have not garnered a comparable level of attention. For instance, evidence for only 4 such interventions to resource efficiency and waste management policies was gathered. Interventions aimed at encouraging sustainable food consumption patterns are 3: it is important to note that most of them targeted food waste, hence they also present a resource efficiency rationale.

The transport domain has not attracted a large number of behavioural interventions (3). Initiatives in this area have thus far mainly revolved around fuel efficiency indicators. Behavioural interventions aimed at enhancing compliance with environmental regulation and at increasing participation in voluntary schemes are also 3, as are applications of BIs to water conservation policy. When it comes to the latter, it is important to note that behavioural insights have attracted attention also in contexts where water scarcity is not an issue.

This report presents and analyses behavioural interventions from a range of countries and institutions. It includes interventions from Australia (2 interventions), Chile (1), Colombia (1), Costa Rica (1), the European Economic and Social Committee (1), the European Commission (7), Israel (3), the Netherlands (1), the Nordic Council (1), Norway (1), South Africa (1), Switzerland (5), the United Kingdom (7) and the United States (3). Some institutions have focused on a single environmentally relevant policy area (e.g. energy in the case of the Behavioural Insights Team in the UK) whereas others have diversified considerably the scope of their BI applications to environmental issues (e.g. the Social and Behavioral Sciences Team in the US and the European Commission). This choice may be due to several factors: political priorities in the environmental policy agenda; ease in monitoring results; economies of scale or learning effects.

Methodologies

As mentioned in the previous chapter, this report analyses behaviourally informed and behaviourally tested policy interventions (see Reader's Guide for definitions of all technical terms). Between these two types, behaviourally informed interventions are less resource-intensive, as they build upon existing behavioural evidence (e.g. from scientific literature or from trials developed in other contexts) rather than on evidence from tailor-made pilot programmes. Behaviourally tested interventions (e.g. field or lab experiments, stated choice experiments) may be more demanding in terms of dedicated human and financial resources, but they have the major advantage of delivering evidence on a specific geographical, cultural and regulatory context. Box 2.1 provides a brief description of commonly used experimental methods to test behavioural interventions.

As illustrated in Figure 2.2, behaviourally informed interventions constitute about 14% of the interventions analysed in this report, whereas the remainder are behaviourally tested interventions, with a clear prevalence of field experiments (56%), followed by stated preference studies such as stated choice experiments (22%) and lab experiments (13%). Some interventions have also built upon multiple methodologies at once.

Box 2.1. **Methodologies for behaviourally tested interventions**

Experiments enable the estimation of a policy's causal effect. The empirical findings of such experiments can inform policy makers, motivating the launch of new policies or changes in existing ones. However, List and Price (2016) argue that the cornerstone for credibly identifying the causal effect of a policy is the construction of the correct counterfactual. The idea behind the establishment of a counterfactual is to compare the impact of the policy of interest on a group that is exposed to it (or, in the experimental jargon, "treated" with it), with its impact on a control group, which is unaffected by the policy intervention.

Harrison and List (2004) argue that "[c]ontrolled" experiments, which include laboratory experiments and field experiments, represent the most convincing method of creating the counterfactual, since they directly construct a control group via randomization" (p. 1014). In fact, randomisation ensures that the individuals or groups of people exposed to the policy to be tested and those instead belonging to the control group are truly comparable (Haynes et al., 2012). Experiments based on the randomised assignment of participants (individuals, households, firms…) to treatment or control groups are called *randomised controlled trials* or, in short, RCTs (see also Haynes et al., 2012; Gertler et al., 2016). According to the type of randomisation process, Charness, Gneezy and Kuhn (2012) distinguish two different types of design:

- "In a ***"within-subject" designed experiment***, each individual is exposed to more than one of the treatments being tested, whether it be playing a game with two different parameter values, being treated and untreated, answering multiple questions, or performing tasks under more than one external stimulus. With such designs, as long as there is independence of the multiple exposures, causal estimates can be obtained by examining how individual behavior changed when the circumstances of the experiment changed.
- In a ***"between-subject" designed experiment***, each individual is exposed to only one treatment. With these types of designs, as long as group assignment is random, causal estimates are obtained by comparing the behavior of those in one experimental condition with the behavior of those in another." (Charness, Gneezy and Kuhn, 2012, p. 1)

Box 2.1. **Methodologies for behaviourally tested interventions** *(continued)*

Likewise, one can talk about *between-group* and *within-group* experimental design, if the randomisation is carried out at the level of *groups* of individuals (e.g. a village, a cohort of students…) rather than at the level of single individuals. According to the experimental context, one can distinguish between:

- ***Laboratory (lab) experiments*** are conducted with volunteer participants in a controlled laboratory facility (Levitt and List, 2009; Noussair and van Soest, 2014).
- ***Field experiments*** are carried out in naturally occurring settings, often with subjects that are unaware of being part of an experiment. Field experiments also include experiments carried out on real online platforms (e.g. e-commerce websites or social networking platforms), which are becoming increasingly popular. Such experiments are denoted in this report by the term ***online field experiments*** (Chen and Konstan, 2015). These should not be confused with experiments carried out on simulated online environments specifically designed for experimental purposes.

Falk and Heckman (2009) state that "the lab offers possibilities to control decision environments in ways that are hard to duplicate with the use of naturally occurring settings". Namely, in this environment, participants take part in the experiments in the presence of examiners. This ensures they carry out the tasks within a given time frame and without external influences. This kind of control is hardly replicable in other types of experiments. On the other hand, Levitt and List (2009) argue that "[f]ield experiments (…) represent a mixture of control and realism usually not achieved in the lab or with uncontrolled data, permitting the analyst to address questions that heretofore were quite difficult to answer." For example, consider the choice of a household appliance among a set of options differing in their energy efficiency rating. When faced with this choice, an individual may act differently in the context of a lab experiment, where usually a fixed budget is provided, and within a field experiment, where one's own budget is at play.

For some of the interventions described in this report, impact evaluation is not based on the randomised assignment of experiment subjects to a treatment or control group. In such cases, causally identifying the impact of the policy intervention requires different methodological approaches based on the analysis of what Levitt and List (2009) call "naturally-occurring data" or "uncontrolled data" (see e.g. Blundell and Costa Dias (2009) for a technical overview of such methodologies and Gertler et al. (2016) for a non-technical one). This approach to causal identification of policy impacts works as long as the policy is introduced as an "exogenous shock", and randomly – in a statistical sense – allocates subjects to control (unaffected by the policy) and treatment (affected by the policy) groups.

An entirely different category of policy interventions involves *stated preference studies*, such as stated choice experiments. In this type of experiments, subjects are presented with hypothetical choice scenarios where they have to select their preferred alternative among a menu of hypothetical options (see also Alpízar, Carlsson and Martinsson, 2003). This type of experiment can be carried out in the context of a survey (with the help of a questionnaire), or in simulated online environments. The aim of this type of studies is to elicit individual preferences and willingness to pay for specific goods or attributes (usually for ones not yet available in the market or for ones where no market exists).

Sources: Alpízar, Carlsson and Martinsson, (2003); Blundell and Costa Dias (2009); Charness, Gneezy and Kuhn (2012); Chen and Konstan (2015); Falk and Heckman (2009); Gertler et al. (2016); Harrison and List (2004); Haynes et al. (2012); Levitt and List (2009); List and Price (2016); Noussair and van Soest (2014).

Figure 2.2. **Methodologies adopted for reviewed BI applications to environmentally relevant policy**

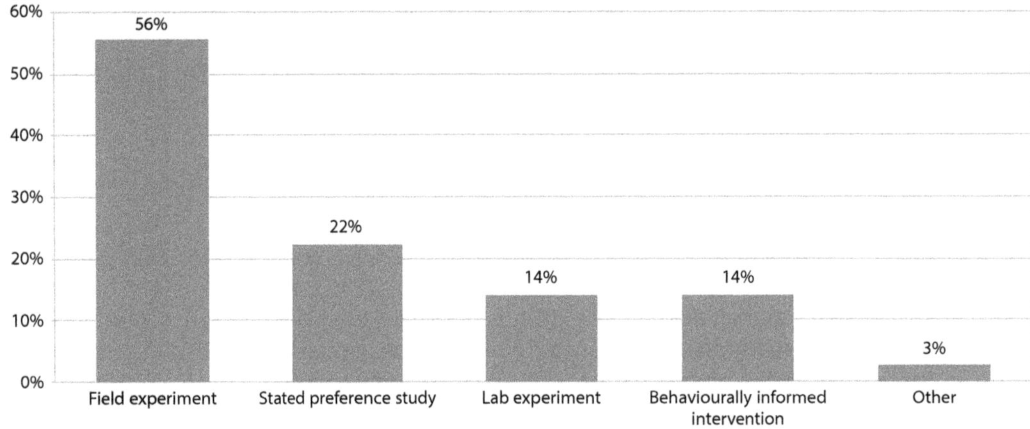

Note: Field experiments also include online field experiments. Stated preference studies include, for example, stated choice experiments carried out in simulated online environments. Some of the 36 BI applications are based on more than one methodology.

Governments and international institutions have typically started to consider the potential of behavioural insights applications through literature reviews, scoping studies and workshops. Some of these reviews have focused on applications to policy making in general (Jonkers and Tiemeijer, 2015; Lunn, 2014; Policy Studies Institute, 2006; Sousa Lourenço et al., 2016; van Bavel et al., 2013; van Bavel, Rodríguez-Priego and Maghiros, 2015). Other governments (Beckenbach et al., 2016; Cabinet Office Behavioural Insights Team, Department of Energy and Climate Change and Department for Communities and Local Government, 2011; Mont, Lehner and Heiskanen, 2014; Oullier and Sauneron, 2011) and international institutions (European Commission, 2012; Mont et al., 2013; UNEP, 2017) instead have focused on the role of behavioural sciences in improving the design and implementation of environmentally relevant policy. This kind of stock-taking exercise can inform environmental policy by helping practitioners diagnose the presence of given behavioural biases underlying environmental issues. Furthermore, it is fundamental to motivate the integration of behavioural insights in environmental policy making. However, this report does not provide a review of such stock-taking publications, instead zooming in on concrete policy applications at the diagnostic and policy design stage: behaviourally informed and behaviourally tested interventions.

Behaviourally informed interventions can be designed to tackle behavioural biases identified following a diagnostic. One such example comes from the United States, where in 2011 the Environment Protection Agency mandated a change in the framing of fuel efficiency labels to include information on the fuel costs associated with car use (see chapter 4). Behavioural insights can also help reshape more effectively government communications: in another example from the United States, behavioural scientists from the Social and Behavioural Sciences Team – a cross-agency group of behavioural scientists and policy makers nested within the Executive Office of the President of the United States – have supported the United States Global Change Research Program (USGCRP) in developing climate indicators that more effectively communicate information to non-scientists (Social and Behavioral Sciences Team, 2016).[2]

Other types of interventions which do not involve empirical impact assessment are surveys. In some cases, surveys have also been used in conjunction with behaviourally tested interventions (e.g. randomised controlled trials) to gather information on participants' characteristics.

While some countries have, for the time being, focused on stock-taking and behaviourally informed interventions (e.g. France, Sweden, Germany), other governments and institutions have moved towards *behaviourally tested interventions.* This has translated into designing, implementing and evaluating the effectiveness of concrete behavioural interventions through field, lab or online experiments. The next section provides an overview of the types of behavioural levers used in such interventions.

Types of behavioural levers

Following the typology presented in Box 1.2, Figure 2.3 provides a snapshot of the distribution of types of levers leveraged in the behavioural interventions reviewed in this report (see Reader's Guide for technical definitions). The majority of interventions (69%) are based on simplification and framing of information. Some of these interventions rely on simplification in order to ease cognitive limitations arising e.g. in the interpretation of particularly complex communications that environment agencies may direct to regulated firms. Others instead increase the salience of future costs and benefits associated with the investment in energy efficient insulation for housing. This can help consumers tackle the short-sightedness hampering such inter-temporal choices.

Changes to the physical environment (17%) have included the introduction of stickers reminding of the importance of water conservation next to water taps, or the installation of real-time in-home displays connected to smart electricity meters to enhance salience of power consumption. *Social norms and comparisons* (17%) have been used to induce energy and water conservation, as well as to prevent littering.

All the other types of behavioural lever have been relatively underexploited. *Green defaults*, for instance, could be further exploited to promote energy conservation by e.g. altering thermostat settings (as tested in an office environment by Brown et al., 2013).

Figure 2.3. **Behavioural levers applied across policy areas**

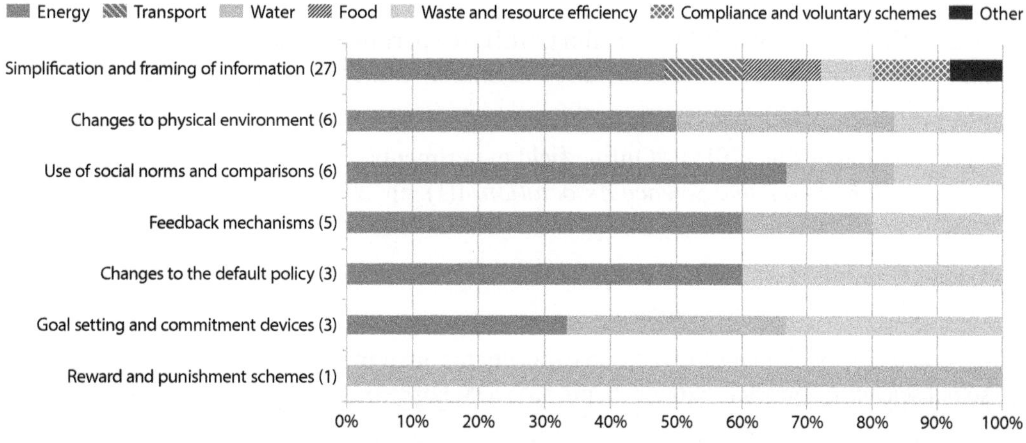

Note: As some of the reviewed BI applications are based on multiple behavioural levers, the total numbers of levers represented in this figure is higher than the total number of BI applications reviewed in this report (36).

Notes

1. The European Commission has adopted both approaches: it has a dedicated team working on the application of behavioural insights across different policy fields (approach 1), which also provides ad-hoc support to policy directorates in the context of framework contracts with specialised, external consortiums (approach 2). While Germany has a specialised unit in the application of behavioural insights at the Office of the Federal Chancellor, projects evaluating the potential contribution of BI applications to environmentally relevant policy are also carried out by the German Environment Agency (UmweltBundesamt).

2. Behaviourally informed interventions can be somewhat harder to detect and document than behaviourally tested interventions, as they are not usually accompanied by impact assessment reports.

References

Alpízar, F., F. Carlsson and P. Martinsson (2003), "Using Choice Experiments for Non-Market Valuation", *Economic Issues*, 8, pp. 83–110.

Beckenbach, F. et al. (2016), *Verhaltensökonomische Erkenntnisse für die Gestaltung umweltpolitischer Instrumente,* Umweltbundesamt, Dessau-Roßlau.

Blundell, R. and M. Costa Dias (2009), "Alternative approaches to evaluation in empirical microeconomics", *Journal of Human Resources*, 44(3), pp. 565–640, http://dx.doi.org/10.1353/jhr.2009.0009.

Brown, Z. et al. (2013), "Testing the effect of defaults on the thermostat settings of OECD employees", *Energy Economics*, 39, pp. 128–134, http://dx.doi.org/10.1016/j.eneco.2013.04.011.

Cabinet Office Behavioural Insights Team, Department of Energy and Climate Change and Department for Communities and Local Government (2011), *Behaviour Change and Energy Use*, London.

Charness, G., U. Gneezy and M. A. Kuhn (2012), "Experimental methods: Between-subject and within-subject design", *Journal of Economic Behavior and Organization*, 81(1), pp. 1–8, http://dx.doi.org/10.1016/j.jebo.2011.08.009.

Chen, Y. and J. Konstan (2015), "Online field experiments: a selective survey of methods", *Journal of the Economic Science Association*, 1(1), pp. 29–42, http://dx.doi.org/10.1007/s40881-015-0005-3.

European Commission (2012), *Green Behaviour,* Future Brief, Science for Environment Policy, Issue 4, October, Brussels.

Falk, A. and J. J. Heckman (2009), "Lab experiments are a major source of knowledge in the social sciences.", *Science*, 326(5952), pp. 535–538, http://dx.doi.org/10.1126/science.1168244.

Gertler, P. J. et al. (2016), *Impact Evaluation in Practice, second edition*, Inter-American Development Bank and World Bank, Washington, DC, http://dx.doi.org/10.1596/978-1-4648-0779-4.

Harrison, G. W. and J. A. List (2004), "Field Experiments", *Journal of Economic Literature*, 42(4), pp. 1009–1055, http://dx.doi.org/10.1257/0022051043004577.

Haynes, L. et al. (2012), *Test, Learn, Adapt: Developing Public Policy with Randomised Controlled Trials*, Cabinet Office Behavioural Insights Team, London.

Jonkers, P. and W. Tiemeijer (2015), *Policymaking Using Behavioural Expertise.* Synopsis of WRR report 92, The Netherlands Scientific Council for Government Policy (WRR), The Hague.

Levitt, S. D. and J. A. List (2009), "Field experiments in economics: The past, the present, and the future", *European Economic Review*, 53(1), pp. 1–18, http://dx.doi.org/10.1016/j.euroecorev.2008.12.001.

List, J. A. and Price, M. K. (2016), "Using Field Experiments in Environmental and Resource Economics", *Review of Environmental Economics and Policy*, 10(2), pp. 206–225, http://dx.doi.org/10.3386/w19289.

Lunn, P. (2014), *Regulatory Policy and Behavioural Economics,* OECD Publishing, Paris, http://dx.doi.org/10.1787/9789264207851-en.

Mont, O. et al. (2013), *Improving Nordic policymaking by dispelling myths on sustainable consumption*, Nordic Council of Ministers, Copenhagen, http://dx.doi.org/10.6027/TN2013-566.

Mont, O., Lehner, M. and Heiskanen, E. (2014), *Nudging – A tool for sustainable behaviour?* Swedish Environmental Protection Agency, Stockholm.

Noussair, C. N. and D. P. van Soest (2014), "Economic Experiments and Environmental Policy: A Review", *Annual Review of Resource Economics*, 6(1), pp. 1–27, http://dx.doi.org/10.1146/annurev-resource-091912-151833.

Oullier, O. and S. Sauneron (2011), "Green nudges: New incentives for ecological behaviours", *Note d'analyse,* Centre d'analyse stratégique, Paris.

Policy Studies Institute (2006), *Designing policy to influence consumers : Consumer behaviour relating to the purchasing of environmentally preferable goods*, Policy Studies Institute, London.

Social and Behavioral Sciences Team (2016), *Social and Behavioral Sciences Team 2016 Annual Report*, Office of Science and Technology Policy, Washington, DC.

Sousa Lourenço, J. et al. (2016), *Behavioural Insights Applied to Policy. European Report 2016*, Science for Policy report, Joint Research Centre, European Commission, Brussels, http://dx.doi.org/10.2760/903938.

UNEP (2017), *Consuming Differently, Consuming Sustainably: Behavioural Insights for Policymaking*, United Nations Environment Programme, Paris.

van Bavel, R. et al. (2013), "Applying Behavioural Sciences to EU Policy-making", *JRC Scientific and Policy Reports,* Joint Research Center, European Commission, Brussels, http://dx.doi.org/10.2788/4659.

van Bavel, R., N. Rodríguez-Priego and I. Maghiros (2015), "Seven Points to Remember when Conducting Behavioural Studies in Support of EU Policy-making", *JRC Scientific and Policy Reports,* Joint Research Center, European Commission, Brussels, http://dx.doi.org/10.2791/743188.

Chapter 3

Using behavioural insights to increase energy conservation and energy efficiency

This chapter analyses the behavioural interventions that have been implemented in the realm of energy policy, highlighting the behavioural biases they tackle and the behavioural levers they build upon. Behavioural interventions in this area have aimed at reducing energy consumption (e.g. providing feedback to consumers), increasing investment in energy efficiency (e.g. framing in a clear and salient way information related to energy efficiency), and encouraging the use of energy from renewable sources (e.g. leveraging green defaults).

The statistical data for Israel are supplied by and under the responsibility of the relevant Israeli authorities. The use of such data by the OECD is without prejudice to the status of the Golan Heights, East Jerusalem and Israeli settlements in the West Bank under the terms of international law.

The majority of applications reviewed in this report are in the realm of energy policy. Indeed, some of the long-standing puzzles in this policy area, such as the low uptake of energy efficient appliances or investments in thermal insulation, can be explained by analysing the behavioural biases driving them. At the same time, some of the current priorities in this policy area (e.g. energy efficiency improvement) require behaviourally motivated policy solutions since their attainment fundamentally rests on behavioural change.

In the energy realm, three types of behaviour are prone to behavioural biases (see Reader's Guide for definitions of all technical terms):

- *Energy consumption*, both at home and at work, is based on *routine, automatic behaviour* rather than on deliberate choices. Energy is an auxiliary good, necessary to consume the services provided by domestic appliances, electronics, etc. Being a routine behaviour, it is strongly dependent on automatic processes.
- On the other hand, deciding to *invest in energy efficiency improvements* (e.g. energy efficient appliances, building insulation), is infrequent for households. Being a rare event, it involves a different decision-making process, in which complex trade-offs between attributes of durable goods are made.
- *Switching energy contract or provider* is another example of effortful choice that is prone to inertia. It requires searching for an alternative deal that better matches one's preferences, and then taking all the required steps to successfully subscribe to it. This is an issue that concerns energy regulators at large, but the focus of this report is on the decision-making process underlying the shift from contracts based on conventional energy sources (e.g. fossil fuels) to contracts based on renewable energy sources.

Promoting energy conservation

Associating specific energy consumption figures to the use of electric appliances or energy-powered services can be complex for consumers. This is due to the fact that energy bills generally present aggregate information (e.g. on the total amount of power consumed throughout a billing period) with a monthly frequency. With conventional energy meters, consumption information is conveyed to consumers with a delay rather than in real time. Infrequent and limited feedback provision prevents users from having a clear picture of the amount of energy required to power a given appliance, as well as of the cost of such an energy service. This issue ultimately leads consumers to optimise their energy consumption given incomplete information. Besides this market failure however, energy consumption choices are also affected by specific behavioural biases:

- *Status-quo bias*: while individual thermostats allow users to adjust heating parameters whenever and as often as they wish, individuals tend to neglect this flexibility and rather stick with the default setting, or adjust it sporadically.
- *Attitude-behaviour gap*: even when considering themselves environmentally concerned, individuals face difficulties adapting their daily behaviour to match their beliefs and preferences. Commitment mechanisms can help, by setting goals for energy conservation and providing regular, timely feedback regarding the advancement towards them. Goals can function as references, thus prompting reference-dependent individuals to overcome their inertia.
- *Framing*: thermostat controls and energy meters are not always designed in an accessible, intuitive way. Furthermore, they are often placed in remote areas of the house, making energy consumption patterns quasi-invisible. Smart thermostats and

smart meters [1] paired with real-time in-home displays can increase the salience and accessibility of information about energy consumption and costs.

Awareness of these biases, related to *bounded rationality* and *bounded willpower,* can help design policy interventions to tackle them and foster energy conservation. Furthermore, there is evidence that behavioural interventions leveraging *bounded self-interest* can also drive energy savings. Since individuals, affected by social norms and comparisons, care about their relative performance with respect to their peers, providing feedback on energy consumption relative to comparable households in the same neighbourhood has proven to be an effective nudge towards energy conservation (Allcott, 2011).

A project that illustrates the potential of behavioural insights applications to encourage energy conservation was developed between 2007 and 2011 by the *British Office of Gas and Electricity Markets* (OFGEM). Involving a number of behavioural levers, ranging from feedback mechanisms to changes to the physical environment and target setting paired with commitment devices, it is an apt opening for this chapter. After providing an overview of this multifaceted set of behavioural interventions, the rest of the chapter zooms in on the most successful ones. The OFGEM-led Energy Demand Research Project included a set of behavioural interventions aimed at studying consumers' response to improved information about their energy consumption. This initiative was undertaken to inform the UK Government's proposed roll-out of smart meters.

The interventions involved over 61 000 households and were delivered by four different energy utilities (AECOM, 2011). The treatments evaluated, individually or in combination, were:

- energy efficiency advice;
- historic energy consumption information (such as comparison of energy consumption with earlier periods);
- benchmarking of the customer's consumption against the consumption of comparable households;
- customer engagement using targets (commitment to reduce consumption);
- smart electricity and gas meters;
- real-time display (RTD) devices that show energy use (including audible usage reduction alarms);
- control of heating and hot water integrated with RTDs;
- financial incentives (including variable tariffs) to either reduce consumption or shift energy use from periods of peak demand to periods of lower demand;
- other digital media for delivering information (web, TV) (AECOM, 2011).

The most successful treatment in reducing energy consumption was found to be the deployment of smart meters coupled with the installation of real-time information displays. In fact, with two exceptions (real-time displays and benchmarking against comparable households' consumption – both leading to energy savings of about 1%), interventions excluding the use of smart meters did not entail any significant energy savings. One of the reasons why smart meters may have delivered important energy savings in this context is that they provide actual feedback on historic consumption, thus enabling consumer learning in the longer run. Furthermore, precise information from smart meters allows energy utilities to bill consumers on the basis of actual consumption rather than estimates.

The project also showed that coupling behavioural levers leads to larger impacts. This is important, even though only separately testing individual behavioural levers allows disentangling their specific impact. For instance, complementing a smart meter with a real-time display is important, and yields energy savings that are 2-4% higher than in the absence of the real-time display. The positive impact related to bundling smart meters and real-time displays may be due to the fact that RTDs make energy consumption more salient, frequent and accurate than meters alone.

While this project provides a good sense of the range of behavioural insights that can inform energy conservation policy, the next sections zoom in on some of these insights, which have been tested in other geographical contexts and through a variety of design choices.

Feedback provision channels: real-time options

The OFGEM project has showcased the potential of feedback mechanisms for energy savings. In a study commissioned by the *Norwegian Water Resources and Energy Directorate* (Ministry of Petroleum and Energy), research and advisory firm VaasaETT reviewed findings from a broad range of *electricity consumption feedback programmes* rolled out in Europe and beyond, for a total of over 90 samples and 30 thousand energy consumers (Norwegian Water Resources and Energy Directorate, 2014).

The review zoomed on the relative effectiveness of such feedback programmes, developed using a variety of feedback channels: real-time, in-home displays (RTDs), informative bills and leaflets, web portals, and mobile applications. It also discussed the extent to which responsiveness to feedback varies across households, and the benefits of automating certain metering functions to deliver higher energy savings. Two of the key take-homes were:

- *Effectiveness of feedback channels:* While all feedback mechanisms have positive impacts on energy conservation, RTDs appear to be the most effective channel. It is important to consider the specificity of each channel prior to choosing one for roll-out, and opting for multiple mechanisms may be the most sensible approach. As mobile applications are a relatively recent feedback mechanism, evidence on their impact is currently insufficient and requires further experimentation.
- *Long-term impact of feedback:* the largest yearly energy savings are delivered by interventions with longer time horizons. In fact, differences in the duration of interventions can explain about 50% of the variation in their impact on energy conservation.

The advantage of performing such a broad-based review is that it allows to draw more general recommendations, on the basis of interventions that have proven to be effective across different geographical, cultural and market contexts. At the same time, the report provides an estimate of potential benefits of extending similar feedback programmes to Norway. It also outlines advantages and disadvantages of each mechanism and suggests how to adapt their roll-out to the Norwegian market.[2]

Alongside smart meters, *smart heating* solutions are emerging in order to promote energy conservation. New generation heating controls allow consumers to turn on/off the heating remotely via a smartphone app, and some models automate heating schedules and set-point temperatures through smart learning algorithms. The *Behavioural Insights Team* is currently evaluating the impact of smart heating controls on household gas consumption in the UK winter heating context, collaborating with a leading heating control manufacturer and a large energy supplier on a two-phase research project. Full results of this ongoing study will be published in 2017 (Behavioural Insights Team, 2016).

Feedback provision via clearer energy bills

The understanding that consumers have of their energy bills is crucial in allowing them to plan and implement energy-saving actions. For this reason, the *Chilean Superintendence of Electricity and Gas* (Superintendencia de Electricidad y Combustibles) and the national agency for consumer protection (Servicio Nacional del Consumidor, SERNAC), together with the innovation hub Laboratorio de Gobierno, are planning a major reshaping of the *content and layout of household energy bills.*

The project started out diagnosing that electricity bills containing unclear or complex expressions do not allow consumers to understand the procedures and the charges associated with energy services. This was followed by a prototyping stage where new bills were designed building upon consumers' feedback. The key changes involved making important information more salient, reducing information overload by synthesising facts in a clear way using simpler terms, and eliminating redundant points. The final prototype for new energy bills is currently being tested through a pilot programme.

In-person guidance and information provision

In co-operation with the *Behavioural Insights Team*, the *UK Department of Energy and Climate Change* (DECC) used a randomised controlled trial to test the *impact of advice and information provision on household energy consumption* (for a more detailed description of the study, see Annex 3.A1). More specifically, the field experiment aimed at testing whether providing households with in-person advice on how to use their thermostat via a trusted messenger (in this case, boiler engineers) led to increased energy savings relatively to written information provision or no intervention (Department of Energy and Climate Change, 2014a).

Thermostat use poses various challenges to consumers, including unintuitive design, difficult to read displays, poorly positioned buttons and controls and overall lack of effective guidance information. This may lead heating users to misuse their heating controls, or to entirely give up their use. This suboptimal thermostat use may lead some particularly vulnerable households to extreme situations such as fuel poverty. This field experiment, rolled out between October 2013 and March 2014, targeted households living in social housing, which were assumed to be particularly prone to these critical situations.

The experiment did not lead to any statistically significant findings; neither guidance nor information provision on thermostat use appeared to generate significant energy savings. Despite no statistical difference in energy use, qualitative analysis following the trial did find that households receiving the treatment reported feeling in more control of their heating versus the control group. Ultimately, given the prevalence of under-heating in social housing dwellings (Department of Energy and Climate Change, 2014a), the impact of the interventions may rather have enabled treated households to live in higher thermal comfort. Testing the same interventions in households prone to higher energy consumption would be informative in order to assess whether they have the potential to deliver energy savings in over-heated dwellings.

These results prevented DECC from extending these interventions to a wider set of British households. Associating qualitative analysis to the quantitative assessment of the intervention's results has enabled DECC to grasp the drivers of energy consumption in this specific subset of the population. This highlights the importance of employing both quantitative and qualitative data collection methods.

Leveraging social comparison to conserve energy in the office environment

While all of the aforementioned interventions tackle household energy consumption, behavioural insights can also inform interventions targeting energy consumption behaviour in office buildings.

The *Government of the Western Cape Province in South Africa* aims at *curbing energy consumption in office buildings*. Since employees are subject to different incentives regarding home and office energy use, ad-hoc behavioural solutions are needed to prompt employees to perform energy savings at work. Several behavioural interventions are being run in office buildings:

- Simply framed information provision via monitors connected to smart meters (on each floor) and via e-mail (reminders and tips).
- Inter-floor competition: leveraging social comparison and status, this intervention pushes for competition among teams of employees working on different floors.
- Identify "champions of energy efficiency" on each office building floor, to act as persons of reference.

While the results of this pilot project are still to be assessed, it is apparent that ongoing interventions on energy conservation at home and in the office differ in behavioural motivations and levers. The former involve simplified energy bills (Chile) and smart thermostat solutions (United Kingdom) and leverage framing and feedback provision, the latter leverage social norms and comparisons as well as framing effects.

Encouraging investment in energy efficiency

Infrequent and limited feedback on energy consumption complicates the understanding of energy requirements to power electric appliances and to heat buildings. This, together with the complexity of an ever-evolving supply of appliances and building insulation options, makes it hard for consumers to understand to what extent their energy expenses could be reduced by investing in energy efficiency.

Given such market features, the significant amount of time and effort required to estimate their long-term financial and environmental benefits can discourage households from investing in energy efficiency improvements (e.g. insulation and retrofit for residential housing). Performing such effortful calculations requires overcoming the status-quo bias driven by:

- *Information overload associated with search costs and effort*: making an investment requires sifting the market for e.g. building insulation for the best deal, which entails search costs. Furthermore, a particularly competitive market, providing a wealth of alternative options to consumers, may actually overwhelm them with an unmanageable quantity of information.
- *Perception of sunk costs*: even though the infrastructure in place – be it roof insulation or incandescent light bulbs – is obsolete and improving its energy efficiency would deliver benefits both in terms of comfort and in terms of financial savings, individuals may still feel that getting rid of functioning assets is a waste, in spite of their cost being sunk.

Investment in energy efficiency improvements is a good example of a decision-making process carrying *intertemporal consequences*. On the one hand, it requires short-term costs, both in terms of upfront expenditures and overcoming non-monetised barriers (e.g. accounting for the various risks and obstacles associated with this process) (Cabinet Office Behavioural Insights Team, Department of Energy and Climate Change and Department for Communities and Local Government, 2011). On the other hand, investing in energy efficiency improvements entails a stream of future energy and monetary savings, which are discounted according to individual patience or impatience.

It is difficult for consumers to understand the long-term benefits that could be reaped if they invested in energy efficiency. Their substantial discounting of future benefits entails that energy efficiency investments are considered as unattractive. This phenomenon is due to impatient consumers' limited willpower, which manifests itself through *myopic preferences.* This kind of short-sightedness complicates the comparison of the short-term costs of energy efficiency investments with their long-term benefits.

Energy efficiency labels can guide consumers towards more energy efficient purchases. *Framing* energy efficiency attributes in a more salient way, making them visible and clear, is an effective way to ensure that they are not left unconsidered at the moment of purchase. Translating figures on expected energy consumption associated with e.g. a certain class of domestic appliances to estimates of monetary costs of operating them can make the benefits of investing in energy efficiency more conspicuous.

Framing cost information to encourage uptake of energy efficient electric appliances

Comparing the short-term purchase costs of energy efficient domestic appliances with the expected long-term savings in energy bills is complex for consumers. If the financial cost of the energy needed to power a certain appliance is not transparent per se, the cumulative costs of operating the appliance throughout its lifetime (lifetime energy cost) are even more complex to calculate.

Introducing information on appliances' lifetime energy costs alongside their standard price tag and energy efficiency label is a way to allow consumers to work out this calculation and compare expected savings across different appliances. With the support of the *Behavioural Insights Team*, the *UK Department of Energy and Climate Change* tested the impact of *adding estimates of lifetime energy costs to the EU energy label for electric appliances* on consumer purchases (for a more detailed description of the study, see Annex 3.A2). The intervention was tested with a field experiment rolled out between September 2013 and April 2014 in a retail chain.

This randomised controlled trial showed that purchases of energy efficient electric appliances can be incentivised by making the energy expenditures incurred throughout the expected lifetime of the appliance more salient. However, this outcome was statistically significant only for high-consumption appliances, such as washer-dryers. For this category of white goods, products sold at treated stores had average expected yearly energy consumption 0.7% lower than products sold at control stores. The consumption differences between high and low energy efficiency washer-dryer models was particularly wide; opting for the more energy efficient ones provided a large potential for savings (Department of Energy and Climate Change, 2014b).

In 2015, the *Swiss Federal Office of Energy* commissioned an online field experiment to test a similar kind of *label including monetary information on the lifetime operating costs of electric appliances,* such as tumble-dryers, vacuum cleaners, freezers and televisions (Schubert and Stadelmann, 2016 – for a more detailed description of the study, see Annex 3.A3). More specifically, this "new" label not only displayed information on the annual electricity costs implied by a given appliance, but also on the relative savings or extra costs for lifetime energy consumption compared with the average appliance in the same class. This framing leveraged loss aversion.

The experiment, carried out on an online retail platform, consisted in exposing consumers alternatively to the "new" label or to the standard EU energy label. The impact of both labels was compared to a pre-experiment baseline situation in which no energy efficiency information was provided to consumers.[3] Consumers who eventually purchased a good on the online retail platform were invited to respond to a questionnaire aimed at understanding the drivers of their purchase decisions.

Overall, these two labels were found to have similar effectiveness in reducing the average annual electricity consumption associated with purchased tumble dryers, leading to an 8-9.6% reduction with respect to the baseline, with the highest reduction being associated with the display of the new labels. On the other hand, neither label influenced the mean annual electricity consumption of purchased freezers.

The label displaying monetary and lifetime costs, however, was less effective than the EU energy label for goods with low annual energy costs such as vacuum cleaners, with the former driving a 4.5% reduction as opposed to a 10.2% reduction associated with the latter. The authors of the study offer two explanations for this result. First, 59% of questionnaire respondents stated that the EU energy label was more comprehensible than the new label, mainly because it was already well-known and looked more familiar. Second, labels displaying lifetime costs may lead consumers to neglect the potential for energy savings from the use of goods with relatively low energy consumption, such as vacuum cleaners. Ultimately, while such labels seem to be more promising in incentivising the purchase of more energy-intensive appliances such as tumble dryers, their potential may be more limited when it comes to less energy-intensive ones, such as vacuum cleaners.

Jointly with the Ministry of Energy, the *behavioural insights team at the Israeli Ministry of Environmental Protection* is currently testing alternative *energy efficiency labels for domestic appliances* building upon the same behavioural insights. The before/after intervention is implemented through a price comparison website. This allows testing whether and to what extent alternative energy efficiency labels drive consumers to purchase more energy efficient refrigerators. The labels differ in the way information on energy efficiency and running costs is framed: information on energy costs over ten years, savings relative to least efficient fridge, or pay-back time of investment in high-efficiency refrigerators.

Framing energy efficiency information to encourage uptake of energy efficient electric appliances

In the context of the impact assessment and revision of its Energy Efficiency directive, the European Commission ordered a cross-country study to assess how various label designs affect consumer understanding and purchase decisions (London Economics and IPSOS, 2014 – for a more detailed description of the study, see Annex 3.A4).

Developed in 2014, the study was based both on a stated choice experiment (carried out on a simulated online platform) and on a field experiment involving respectively over 5000 and 500 consumers in 9 European countries (Czech Republic, France, Italy, Norway, Poland, Portugal, Romania, Slovenia and United Kingdom). It showed that labels with alphabetic scales were generally more intuitive and thus better understood by consumers than labels with numeric scales, and were ultimately more effective, leading to more choices of energy efficient products.

Furthermore, the experiment showed that such intuitive and effective label design is more important to inform consumers who are generally inattentive to energy consumption than energy-conscious ones. In fact, energy-conscious consumers are aware of energy efficiency indicators, understand them easily and take them into account in their choices, regardless of label designs. In contrast, improving the intuitiveness of label design (e.g. basing energy efficiency indicators on letters rather than numeric scales) can significantly increase the awareness of consumers who would not necessarily consider energy efficiency in their appliance purchases and drive them towards more energy efficient choices.

Online shopping behaviour is different from its traditional retail counterpart in a number of dimensions. First, switching between retailers is essentially immediate and costless. Second, because of the wealth of options available, consumers tend to simplify their decision-making process using a two-step approach: the comparison tools offered by most retail websites allow consumers to narrow down their pool of considered alternatives to a manageable number, comparing goods along the same criteria. Once this is done, choosing the best option among the shortlisted ones is relatively easier. Finally, on online retail platforms, room for information provision is relatively limited in comparison with traditional shopping outlets.

Because of these differences, designing energy efficiency labels for the online purchase environment could help consumers to choose more energy efficient appliances. In 2014, the Consumers, Health, Agriculture and Food Executive Agency (CHAFEA) followed up on the previous study and, on behalf of the European Commission, ordered an impact assessment of a range of new label designs (ECORYS, Tilburg University and GfK, 2014 – see also Annex 3.A5). It was rolled out in 10 EU countries (France, Germany, Greece, Ireland, Italy, the Netherlands, Poland, Portugal, Romania and Sweden), involving over 11 700 consumers.

Using a stated choice experiment carried out on a simulated online platform, the study assessed the relative effectiveness of various label designs in inducing consumers to choose more energy efficient appliances (washing machines, refrigerators, televisions and lightbulbs). At the same time, the experiment aimed at understanding when it is best to expose consumers to energy labels. More specifically, it tested whether label exposure led consumers to more energy efficient purchases: a) when they were browsing the retailer's website to select a subset of products matching their needs (set formation stage) or b) when the good to purchase was selected from the relevant subset of products (final choice stage).

Participants were exposed either to the first or to the second experiment. Within each experiment, four different labels were tested: i) a label indicating only the energy efficiency class of a good (e.g. "A"); ii) a label additionally indicating the class indicator and its meaning (e.g. "energy efficiency A"); iii) a label including a frame of reference (e.g. "A B C D E F G" rather than just "A" to represent a product with energy efficiency class A) and iv) a pictogram label, conveying both the meaning of energy efficiency and the complete scale of energy efficiency classes (labels are pictured in Annex 3.A5). These were "simplified" labels, smaller and more concise than the more detailed EU energy label for household appliances normally shown in physical stores. To enable comparisons of the influence of simplified labels on individual behaviour with the influence of the EU energy label, a group of participants was also exposed to the latter at the final choice stage. Control groups in the two experiments were defined as follows: in the experiment looking at the set formation stage, the control group was exposed to no information on energy efficiency; in the experiment dealing with the final choice stage, the control group was exposed to non-prominent information on energy efficiency (e.g. the energy efficiency class was written in the same font as other product attributes).

In both experiments, all proposed simplified labels were found to lead to a higher consideration of more energy efficient products than the information provided to the control groups. Among simplified labels, the best performing one was label (iii), i.e. the one including a frame of reference. At the set formation stage, label (iii) led to the most efficient product being selected on average 61% of the time as opposed to 51% of the time in the control group. At the final choice stage, the margin was lower: the most efficient product was selected 68% of the time when label (iii) was shown as opposed to 65% of the time in the control group. In that experiment, all four simplified labels outperformed the standard EU energy label normally shown in physical stores. Ultimately, the findings of the study suggest that simplifying energy efficiency information on product labels presented online – especially in the early stage of the choice-making process – can lead to more energy efficient purchases.

Framing the costs and benefits of household retrofit to increase their salience

In conjunction with *Plymouth University*, the *Behavioural Insights Team* recently completed a randomised controlled trial aimed at *encouraging investment in residential building insulation using thermal imaging* (Behavioural Insights Team, 2016). Thermal images allow visualising the flow of heat, spotting heat loss due to drafts. In an attempt to raise awareness of the benefits of insulation, the city council of Plymouth, UK, sent three different types of letters to residents of the municipality, announcing public grants for households interested in retrofitting their homes. The first type of letter showed a thermal image of an uninsulated home, with salient heat loss; the second type of letter showed, side by side, an insulated and an uninsulated home. The control group instead received a plain, text-only letter informing them of grant possibilities. The objective of thermal images was to make the cost of poor building insulation clearly visible, thus prompting the uptake of grants to invest in insulation. However, the redesigned letters including thermal images led to fewer letter recipients inquiring about grant possibilities relative to the control group. This may be due to recipients considering thermal images irrelevant for their case (e.g. possibly because they portrayed a similar building rather than precisely their own home), or not understanding them properly.

While this study aimed at increasing the salience of the costs due to missing insulation (through telling thermal images of leaking heat), increasing the salience of potential benefits connected to retrofitting buildings can also help consumers. Enhancing energy efficiency labelling or certificates for buildings can be a way to increase the salience of expected benefits (e.g. providing estimates of expected energy savings) and to outline specific actions needed to reap them (e.g. loft insulation, double glazing).

In this respect, the *Social and Behavioural Sciences Team* nested within the White House has paired with the *US Department of Energy* in order to *design and assess the impact of the Home Energy Score*. The score assesses residential buildings' energy efficiency profiles and provides recommendations for improving them in order to reap energy savings (Social and Behavioral Sciences Team, 2016). This project is still ongoing; hence, the impact of this specific intervention has not yet been empirically assessed.

Leveraging social norms and inertia to encourage the uptake of building insulation

Behavioural insights can inform environmental policy design by motivating tweaks to conventional instruments such as financial incentive schemes. For example, leveraging social norms, policy makers can design group financial incentives that are increasing in the number of group members making a certain target investment (e.g. the uptake of building insulation). Another example of behaviourally motivated variation of standard subsidies relies on easing or removing the non-financial burdens preventing the target investment (e.g. lack of time, perceived hassle and disruption), rather than solely subsidising the latter. The *Behavioural Insights Team* (BIT) has tested similar behavioural tweaks to financial incentives in order to encourage investment in building insulation in residential housing.

In autumn 2011, the BIT investigated the *impact of social norms on the uptake of insulation for housing*. Recognising that people tend to adopt the behaviour of others and align with others' opinions and judgements, this policy intervention leveraged the importance that social networks have in the adoption of green behaviours and in the uptake of environmentally sustainable investment.

More specifically, social norms were exploited by proposing group incentives to insulation purchasers, in the form of discounts that increased with the number of consumers opting in. Instead of engaging consumers individually, this incentive scheme built upon the sense of community through which environmentally friendly (or unfriendly) behaviours can spread. The more community members participated in the scheme, the higher the discount each investor obtained on their purchase.

The effectiveness of this intervention was tested with a randomised controlled trial in two different British towns (Greater London area) with the co-operation of a home improvement retailer: in the treated area, households purchasing insulation were offered the group incentive scheme, while no incentives were offered in the control area.

The intervention did not result in any significant effect of group incentives on insulation uptake. For this reason, the extension of this type of discount to a broader set of eligible British households was not pursued. This result prompted the BIT to study the impact of outstanding hurdles to the uptake of insulation even in the presence of financial incentives. One such barrier is that installing thermal insulation in buildings requires effortful preparatory tasks, e.g. loft clearance in the case of loft insulation. The cost associated with the required immediate effort may seem disproportionate relative to the expected future benefits of energy savings and lower bills. This kind of investment is constrained by inertia and resistance to change on the one hand, and by myopia due to high discounting of future benefits on the other.

The *UK Department of Energy and Climate Change*, together with the *Behavioural Insights Team*, ran a randomised controlled trial in spring 2012 to assess the impact of a *"hassle removal"* package offering subsidised loft clearance alongside insulation (see also Annex 3.A6). The objective of the package was to nudge investment in household retrofit and insulation improvement. This randomised controlled trial tested whether proposing packages including loft clearance and insulation (either at full cost or at a discount) would increase the installation of loft insulation with respect to offers mentioning insulation only.

While there was some indication that reducing the hassle factor increased the uptake of loft insulation (particularly at a discount), it was not possible to conclude with certainty because overall participation in the trial was low (Department of Energy and Climate Change, 2013). This did not allow a disentangling of the different barriers to uptake (e.g. physical limitations with the property, motivation of the household…).

Understanding consumers' perception of energy efficiency labels

A 2016 study commissioned by the *Swiss Federal Office of Energy* analysed *consumers' information search behaviour in the context of product choice* (e.g. purchase of electric appliances – for a more detailed description of the study, see Annex 3.A7). Through a set of three stated choice experiments and a lab eye-tracking experiment, the study aimed at understanding the extent to which consumers dwelled on energy efficiency and energy consumption information provided on product labels, and what their understanding of these indicators was (Wächter, Sütterlin and Siegrist, 2015a, 2015b, 2016). When asked to pick the appliance with the lowest energy consumption, consumers often tended to base their decision solely on the energy efficiency rating (e.g. between A+++ and D in EU energy labels), without comparing the actual information on energy consumption provided in the label.

Consumers are thus prone to what the authors of the study call the "energy efficiency fallacy", that is, they are prone to infer the amount of energy required to power appliances from their energy efficiency rating. This phenomenon is, at least to some extent, a consequence of the relative salience and higher consumer awareness of the letter-based energy efficiency rating as compared with information on actual energy consumption. Hence, consumers use the former indicator as a heuristic for the latter. This can be misleading as energy efficiency ratings are relative indicators, whereas information on energy consumption allows getting a sense of the actual energy requirements of an appliance in absolute terms. Ultimately, by considering solely the energy efficiency rating, consumers may end up purchasing appliances which are very energy efficient with respect to other goods in their class (e.g. televisions with the same screen size), yet energy intensive in absolute terms (e.g. televisions with smaller screen sizes).

Encouraging the use of energy from renewable sources

The behavioural phenomenon of inertia is apparent in the choice of energy contracts. Because searching for alternative contracts (or providers altogether) is burdensome, consumers tend to adhere to the default option provided by energy retailers. If the policy objective is to increase the uptake of electricity contracts based on renewable energy, this default bias can be addressed by making such contracts the default choice. At the moment of contract choice, consumers should be signalled whether and to what extent these contracts entail higher costs than their counterparts based on electricity from fossil fuels or nuclear energy.

Through an incentivised laboratory experiment,[4] a study financed by the *Swiss Federal Office of Energy* analysed the effects of such *changes in default options*, whereby electricity retailers offer renewable energy via default contracts (Ghesla, forthcoming – for a more detailed description, see Annex 3.A8). In a lab setting, participants were exposed to three treatments: the baseline one, where they actively chose the proportion of renewable and conventional energy within their electricity contract, and two different default contracts, based either entirely on conventional energy or on renewable energy (respectively, "grey" and "green" defaults). Nonetheless, even when they were proposed a default contract, participants could choose to create their own energy mix instead, indicating their desired proportion of renewable and conventional electricity. This "contract change", however, required additional effort. Alternative scenarios were modelled: while conventional electricity was always cheaper than renewable electricity, the latter could be associated with a low (CHF 0.01 to CHF 0.03 per kWh) or high (between CHF 0.04 and CHF 0.2 per kWh) price premium with respect to the former.

When the renewable energy price premium was low, the study showed that green defaults led participants to choose significantly more renewable electricity than in the active choice and grey default situations. For example, with a price premium of CHF 0.01 per kWh, the mean share of green electricity in contracts reached 86% under a green default, 67% under active choice and 71% under a grey default. As shifting away from a default situation entailed effort, consumers tended to stick with the default contract whenever they assessed the benefit of shifting was lower than the cost of doing so. In this kind of price scenario, green defaults seem to induce a higher consumption of renewable energy than the one seemingly desired by consumers. Conversely, if the price premium associated with renewable electricity was high, there was no statistically significant difference between the mean share of renewable energy driven by active choice and by green default contracts, while grey defaults, intuitively, led to a significantly lower demand for green electricity than active choice. Thus, in this price scenario, the outcome of the green default option matched that of active choice. It seems that energy regulators should induce consumers to actively choose the energy mix that best suits them, removing where needed the market barriers that oust this. The final outcome of consumer choice of electricity contracts, however, depends on their energy literacy of consumers and on their ability to navigate the power market.

While changes to default options can be one way to promote the adoption of renewable energy sources, another ongoing project financed by the *Swiss Federal Office of Energy* considers the *impact of social norms in increasing the uptake of renewables by both households and firms*. More specifically, it compares the impact of alternative policy measures – traditional market-based tools (e.g. subsidies), communication/marketing campaigns and behaviourally motivated social marketing campaigns leveraging peer effects – on the probability of investing in solar energy installations. As this project is ongoing, it has not yet undergone empirical assessment.

Conclusion on energy conservation and energy efficiency

A fundamental reason behind the wealth of behavioural interventions on energy efficiency and consumption is that it is relatively straightforward to measure their outcomes. For example, the success of an intervention aimed at curbing household energy consumption can be assessed through the change in consumption of electricity (in kWh) before and after the intervention, comparing a treatment with a control group. As will be discussed in the following chapters, effective and intuitive indicators are not necessarily as easily available when it comes to, inter alia, waste reduction or transport mode change.

In terms of the design of interventions on energy, the main trend observed is towards increasing the salience of energy consumption and efficiency indicators, mainly through better designed energy efficiency labels (leveraging simplification and framing of information) but also through smart meters and thermostats (changes to the physical environment). Providing feedback, changing default options and benchmarking energy consumption against peers – thus exploiting social norms and comparisons – are also popular interventions. The main methodologies behind behaviourally tested applications in this policy area are field experiments (13 applications) followed by stated preference studies (3) and lab experiments (2). Two behaviourally informed applications are also presented.

Evidence from completed interventions should be interpreted bearing in mind the specific context in which the various experiments were carried out. However, some general policy-relevant results could be pointed out.

Energy efficiency labels do seem to induce consumers to purchase more energy efficient appliances. However, not all types of labels do so, and design choices are crucial for ensuring that a label's meaning is well understood by consumers. This result has motivated the European Commission's proposed revision of energy efficiency labels, put forward in summer 2015 (European Commission, 2015). At the same time, the European Commission has been exploring possibilities to enrich energy efficiency labels with information on other aspects of product environmental footprint, such as e.g. carbon emissions (Annex 3.A9 describes a behavioural intervention implemented to test two variants of such environmental footprint labels).

There is evidence that consumers are prey to the so-called "energy efficiency fallacy", whereby they use information on an appliance's energy efficiency rating as heuristic for its energy consumption. This can be misleading as energy efficiency ratings are relative indicators, whereas information on energy consumption provides an estimate of an appliance's energy requirements in absolute terms. Ultimately, by considering solely the energy efficiency rating, consumers may end up purchasing appliances which are very energy efficient with respect to other goods in their class, yet energy intensive in absolute terms (Wächter et al., 2016).

Complementing energy efficiency labels with estimates of lifetime running costs of appliance use can further help consumers in turning their choice towards more energy efficient white goods (Department of Energy and Climate Change, 2014b; Schubert and Stadelmann, 2016). However, while both studies reviewed in this chapter have shown promising results of such labels for electric appliances with high energy consumption (e.g. washer-dryers), there is evidence that they provide insufficient incentives when it comes to purchasing less energy-intensive appliances such as vacuum cleaners (Schubert and Stadelmann, 2016). While the usefulness of adding estimates of lifetime running costs to energy labels has also been demonstrated in scientific research (Kallbekken et al., 2013), to the best of our knowledge it has not yet prompted policy action in this direction (cf. Chapter 4 for fuel efficiency labels).

Incentives for investment in measures to increase energy efficiency (e.g. by installing home insulation) building upon social norms and "hassle removal" did not prove to have statistically significant results in the British context. Similarly, providing guidance and information on thermostat use did not yield statistically significant impacts (Department of Energy and Climate Change, 2013, 2014a). Two lessons can be drawn from these findings. First, it is worth repeating that conclusions from pilot programmes carried out in very specific contexts cannot necessarily be generalised. Second, non-statistically significant results can impact policy-making too. Testing interventions prior to mainstreaming new policies to the entire population has prevented the British government from incurring sizeable public expenditures for measures which have not proven to be effective. Preceding policy implementation with this kind of ex-ante assessment can ensure public spending is directed to impactful interventions.

Providing feedback on energy consumption via smart meters drives energy savings across households (AECOM, 2011). It is important to pair smart meters with visible devices, such as real-time information displays, in order to make energy consumption patterns salient.

There is limited evidence on the impact of changes in defaults on consumers' choice of electricity contracts differing in the energy mix they propose (i.e. share of renewable and conventional energy). The findings of Ghesla (forthcoming) suggest that the outcomes of green defaults – as opposed to active choice of the energy mix – very much depend on the relative prices of conventional and renewable energy. It would be useful to further investigate the impact of green defaults on consumer choices of energy contracts, using larger and more representative samples of individuals.

Annex 3.A1

Guidance, information provision and energy savings – UK

Context	
Who?	Department of Energy and Climate Change (DECC) in partnership with the Behavioural Insights Team, Newcastle City Council, Your Homes Newcastle (social housing) and Building and Commercial Enterprises (engineering firm for boiler checks).
Where?	Newcastle, UK
When?	October 2013 – May 2014
Why?	This intervention investigated whether providing households with guidance on thermostat use via a trusted messenger eventually led to increased energy savings relatively to information provision or to no intervention at all.
Behavioural intervention	
Environmental policy objective	Encourage conservation of resources
Behavioural issue	Status-quo bias
Behavioural lever	Changes to the default policy

Evaluation of the intervention: methodology

Relevant population: Social housing tenants in Newcastle.

Sample size and sampling method(s): 1556 households, sampled among Newcastle social housing tenants.

Method: field experiment designed as a parallel randomised controlled trial: testing of the interventions occurs in parallel.

The experiment tested a change in default policy: rather than providing only a routine check on boilers, boiler engineers started providing guidance and/or information on thermostat use to the households they visited.

The sample was divided into three groups:

- *Advice treatment*: boiler engineers provide advice on efficient boiler usage (312 households),
- *Information treatment*: boiler engineers leave an information leaflet (570 households).
- *Control*: boiler engineers visit the household for the standard check but provide no guidance/information (674 households).

Treatment was randomly assigned in two ways: engineers were randomly assigned to their specific duties (perform boiler check and provide advice/information leaflet/ no intervention) and households were randomly assigned to the engineers who were to perform their boiler check.

Units of measurement: Percentage change in individual household gas consumption (before/after the intervention).

Findings

None of the interventions had a significant effect on energy use.

Thus, the trial did not provide evidence supportive of guidance and information provision as effective tools for reducing gas consumption in social housing. However, follow-up qualitative interviews provided evidence that interventions led tenants to reach higher thermal comfort in their homes.

Source

Department of Energy and Climate Change (2014a), *Advice on how to use heating controls: Evaluation of a trial in Newcastle*, DECC, London, https://www.gov.uk/government/uploads/system/uploads/attachment_data/file/349855/decc_heating_controls_report.pdf.

Behavioural Insights Team (2015), *The Behavioural Insights Team Update Report 2013-2015*, Behavioural Insights Ltd., London, www.behaviouralinsights.co.uk/wp-content/uploads/2015/07/BIT_Update-Report-Final-2013-2015.pdf.

Annex 3.A2

Perception of cost savings related to the use of energy efficient white goods – UK

Context	
Who?	Department of Energy and Climate Change (DECC) in partnership with the Behavioural Insights team and the retail chain John Lewis.
Where?	Several locations, UK
When?	September 2013 – June 2014
Why?	To analyse the impact of different types of energy efficiency labelling on purchases of energy efficient appliances. More specifically, the intervention tested a variation of the EU energy efficiency label by including in it information on lifetime electricity costs of electric appliances.
Behavioural intervention	
Environmental policy objective	Promote private investment in more efficient technologies
Behavioural issue	Attitude-behaviour gap; status-quo bias; myopic preferences. A relatively small number of purchases of energy efficient appliances underline a discrepancy between consumers' stated intentions to reduce expenditures on energy and their behaviour at the moment of purchase, where energy efficiency is only one among various product attributes under scrutiny.
Behavioural lever	Simplification and framing of information

Evaluation of the intervention: methodology

Relevant population: Customers of John Lewis retail shops for home appliances throughout the UK.

Sample size and sampling method(s):

The sample consisted of customers of 38 stores of John Lewis.

The sample was stratified by store location: town-centre and out-of-town stores. This segmentation choice was made as the two types of stores target different groups of consumers.

Method: field experiment, designed as cluster parallel randomised controlled trial.

This means that randomisation was clustered at store level rather than at the individual consumer level.

Stores were randomised into:

- Treatment group: 19 stores, where white goods information tags reported lifetime electricity costs on top of EU energy label.
- Control group: 19 stores, where white goods were only tagged with the standard product information and EU energy label.

The experiment involved four types of appliances: washing machines, washer dryers, and two types of tumble driers (vented and condensed).

Units of measurement:

Percentage change in average amount of energy consumed (in kWh/year, calculations based on type-approval energy efficiency values) by the appliances sold within each product category.

Findings

The impact of including full lifetime electricity costs in energy efficiency labels was positive for washer-dryers: on average, products sold at treated stores had average yearly energy consumption 0.7% lower than products sold at control stores (washer-dryers sold in treated stores consumed on average 6.64kWh/year less energy than their counterparts sold in control stores). This impact was statistically significant at the 10% level ($p \leq 0.1$). No significant impact was detected for washing machines and dryers. This may be due to the important difference in running costs between low and high efficiency washer-dryers, while this difference is less marked for the other white goods analysed.

The impact seems to be more pronounced for out-of-city stores than for urban ones.

Two caveats:

- It was impossible to disentangle the impact of information on lifetime electricity costs of appliances from the impact of training staff to provide advice in interpreting labels.
- Because the experiment did not involve any in-store survey with consumers, the reasons behind certain findings (e.g. no statistically significant impact of labels including lifetime costs on purchases of washing machines and dryers) could not be pinned down with certainty.

The cost-effectiveness of this intervention was evaluated through a broad cost-benefit analysis, based on the extrapolation of the statistically significant results of the trial to sales of washer-dryers over one year to two broader scenarios: 1) all John Lewis stores in the UK and 2) all appliance stores in the UK.

First, this showed that extending the use of the new type of labels to washer-dryers throughout the whole retail chain (John Lewis) would entail costs of around GBP 1 000 (in present value terms) to design labels and train employees. The net present value of social benefits associated with the intervention would be around GBP 47 000, thanks to GBP 48 000 benefits from avoided emissions. The retail chain decided to continue the pilot with new labels, potentially adapting them to include yearly energy costs rather than lifetime energy costs to improve readability.

Second, extending the intervention to label all washer-dryers throughout all appliance shops in the UK would deliver a social NPV estimated at GBP 1.7 million throughout their lifetime. This consists of GBP 1.8 million benefits due to avoided emissions and GBP 0.1 million in costs to business.

Source

Department of Energy and Climate Change (2014b), *Evaluation of the DECC/John Lewis energy labelling trial*, DECC, London, https://www.gov.uk/government/uploads/system/uploads/attachment_data/file/350282/John_Lewis_trial_report_010914FINAL.pdf.

Annex 3.A3

Drivers of the purchase of energy efficient durables – Switzerland

Context	
Who?	Swiss Federal Office of Energy, study developed by researchers at ETH Zürich.
Where?	Switzerland
When?	June-December 2015
Why?	This intervention assesses the role of two energy efficiency labels, the EU energy efficiency label and a newly-designed label, on consumer purchase decisions.
Behavioural intervention	
Environmental policy objective	Promote private investment in more efficient technologies
Behavioural issue	Attitude-behaviour gap; status-quo bias; myopic preferences. A relatively small number of purchases of energy efficient appliances underline a discrepancy between consumers' stated intentions to reduce expenditures on energy and their behaviour at the moment of purchase, where energy efficiency is only one among various product attributes under scrutiny.
Behavioural lever	Simplification and framing of information

Evaluation of the intervention: methodology

Relevant population: Consumers of energy-using durable goods in Switzerland.

Sample size and sampling method(s): The sample consisted of the consumers who purchased the products sold on the online platform participating in the experiment between June 2015 and December 2015.

The sample size varied per type of product sold:

- Freezers: 330
- Vacuum cleaners: 865
- Tumble dryers: 128
- Televisions: 1416

Method

This study built on a three-fold approach.

Part 1 of the study provided a *literature review.*

Part 2 assessed whether and to what extent there is an *energy efficiency gap* related to energy-using durables purchased in Switzerland. This was done by matching pairs of otherwise identical products differing in energy use and purchase price, and calculating the discounted total lifetime cost of each option (based on purchase costs, energy costs and individual discount rates). An energy efficiency gap exists if the energy efficient product is cheaper – in terms of total lifetime costs – than its less efficient counterpart, yet it is not purchased. The authors gathered data on appliances' list prices from Swiss manufacturers' and calculated the discounted total lifetime cost associated to a number of appliances: they found that the energy efficient product was never the most convenient option in this subset of retailer-product combinations. In contrast, when using online shop prices, they found evidence that choosing the energy efficient product was often the economically rational choice because of lower discounted total lifetime cost relative to less energy efficient counterparts.

Part 3 used an *online field experiment* to test the impact of two types of energy efficiency labels on the purchase of energy-using durable goods. This was carried out on an online retail platform and involved goods with high variability in energy consumption and energy efficiency classes, i.e. tumble dryers, vacuum cleaners, freezers and televisions.

The labels tested in the field experiment were:

- Treatment 1: the EU energy label
- Treatment 2: monetary costs and lifetime-oriented label. This label displayed:
  - The annual electricity costs of a product on a colour-coded scale from green (low electricity costs) to red (high electricity costs). The scale gave a sense of the minimum and maximum energy expenditures for products in the same class (e.g. products with the same size/capacity).
  - A relative assessment of a product's lifetime energy costs with the average appliance in the same class: this was expressed as a gain or a loss relative to the average.

The treatment allocation was designed as follows: starting in June 2015 and for six months, the labels associated with treatment 1 and 2 were alternatively shown for periods of four weeks alongside the product description on the partner website. Both labels were thus displayed on the website for a total of 12 weeks (3 times 4 weeks), which allows testing for seasonal effects.

Impacts were measured relative to baseline data from product sales in the 12 weeks preceding the experiment (end of March 2015 to mid-June 2015), where no information on energy efficiency or consumption was shown.

The field experiment was followed by a survey. Information on customers was gathered via online questionnaires sent to participants after their purchase. These included questions on "purchase motives, expectations on product lifetime, perception of energy labels, environmental attitudes and energy literacy" (Schubert and Stadelmann, 2016, p. 32). Customers who responded to the questionnaire were rewarded for their participation with a gift card for the online shop. A total of 469 questionnaires were received.

Units of measurement

- Share of energy efficient products in the purchases made during each treatment period.
- Average energy consumption of products sold during each treatment period.

Findings

Regarding the *share of energy efficient products* sold during each treatment period, both labels were found to lead consumers towards the purchase of a higher proportion of energy efficient vacuum cleaners, tymble dryers and freezers relatively to the baseline period. The impact on television sales could not be assessed because of a lack of data from the baseline period.

Results on the *average energy consumption* of purchased products were instead less homogeneous across products. Overall, the EU energy efficiency label and the monetary costs and lifetime-oriented label seemed to have similar effects on the average annual electricity consumption of tumble dryers and freezers. Tagging goods with the EU energy label drove a statistically significant reduction in the mean annual electricity consumption of tumble dryers by 8% with respect to the baseline situation, while tagging them with the monetary costs and lifetime-oriented label drove a reduction of 9.6%. The two labels were found to be equally ineffective in encouraging the sales of more energy efficient freezers.

The monetary and lifetime-oriented label, however, was shown to be less effective than the EU energy label for goods with low annual energy costs such as vacuum cleaners. For this category of goods, the EU label led to a -10.2% reduction in mean annual electricity use of purchased vacuum cleaners with respect to the baseline, whereas the figure was -4.5% when consumers were shown the new energy label.

This may be explained by looking at answers to the online questionnaire, which showed that the majority of consumers preferred the EU energy label, as they were more familiar with it. Furthermore, because the annual electricity costs of using vacuum cleaners are very low (on average 7.20 CHF), the new labels based on monetary impacts may lead consumers to neglect the potential for energy efficiency improvements from such low-consumption goods.

Note that the purchase of freezers was associated with a "volume effect", whereby both labels led to purchases of appliances that were both more energy efficient and larger. The authors suggest that "[a]n approach to eliminate the volume-effect could be to rate products only based on their absolute electricity consumption and not on electricity consumption relative to the size of the product (as done by the EU Energy Label). For the newly designed energy label, the volume-effect might be eliminated by arranging products of all sizes on one single range of annual electricity costs" (Schubert and Stadelmann, 2016, p. 46).

Finally, the study compared the average energy consumption per category of sold products in the period in which the EU energy label was shown and in the period in which the new label was shown. The only products for which there was evidence of a stastistically significant difference in the average energy consumption of sales were vacuum dryers.

Source

Schubert, R. and M. Stadelmann (2016), *Energy-Using Durables: Driving Forces of Purchase Decisions*, report for the Swiss Federal Office of Energy, Bern, www.bfe.admin.ch/php/modules/enet/streamfile.php?file=000000011364.pdf&name=000000291123.

Annex 3.A4

Energy efficiency labelling and consumer behaviour – European Commission

	Context
Who?	Study realised by London Economics and IPSOS on behalf of the European Commission.
Where?	According to the phase of the project, a total of 9 European countries are involved: Czech Republic, France, Italy, Norway, Poland, Portugal, Romania, Slovenia and United Kingdom.
When?	2014
Why?	The intervention investigated the impact of alternative energy label designs on consumer understanding and the choice of home appliances.
	Behavioural intervention
Environmental policy objective	Promote private investment in more efficient technologies
Behavioural issue	Attitude-behaviour gap; status-quo bias; myopic preferences. A relatively small number of purchases of energy efficient appliances underline a discrepancy between consumers' stated intentions to reduce expenditures on energy and their behaviour at the moment of purchase, where energy efficiency is only one among various product attributes under scrutiny.
Behavioural lever	Simplification and framing of information

Evaluation of the intervention: methodology

Relevant population: Consumers from the Czech Republic, France, Italy, Norway, Poland, Portugal, Romania, Slovenia and the United Kingdom.

Sample size and sampling method(s)

- *Online stated choice experiment*: 5012 respondents (about 1000 each from France, Italy and the United Kingdom; about 500 each from the Czech Republic, Norway, Poland and Romania).
- *Field experiment*: 500 respondents (125 each from the Czech Republic, France, Slovenia and Portugal). Participants were recruited both in-store and on the street.

Method: The study comprised a literature review and the aforementioned two experiments.

The literature review collected information about consumer responses to and understanding of various energy labelling schemes.

The experimental work aimed at assessing the impact of different energy label designs on consumption choices and on consumers' understanding of the provided information. It was carried out in two phases:

- An incentivised *stated choice experiment* in a simulated online environment. Participants in this experiment were rewarded with higher payoffs the more energy efficient products they picked.
- A *field experiment* in retail stores.

Stated choice experiment

The products involved in this experiment were televisions, washing machines and light bulbs.

The tested labels were:

a. closed alphabetic scale (A to G scale) – this was the baseline treatment;

b. closed numeric scale (30 to 100);

c. open numeric scale (0 to 110, with grey bars for energy efficiency of past and future technologies, respectively indicated with scores lower than 30 and higher than 100);

d. closed numeric scale with a benchmark marker showing current best available technology;

e. closed reversed numeric scale (7 to 1).

Exposure to labels was randomised.

Participants were exposed either to a choice experiment (eliciting their favourite option between two products differing in energy efficiency and other attributes) or to a bidding experiment (eliciting their willingness to pay for more energy efficient products).

Field experiment

The tested labels were:

a. an A+++ to D label;

b. an A to G label;

c. a numeric label with ratings for possible future technologies shown in grey;

d. a reverse numeric label (9 to 3).

Participants were asked to consider making two hypothetical purchase choices: one regarding televisions and one regarding washing machines. Exposure to labels was randomised. Following the choice statement, participants were surveyed in order to assess their understanding of labels and preferences regarding energy efficiency.

Units of measurement

Impact of labels on product choice:

- Proportion of respondents that chose the most energy efficient appliance among the proposed ones.
- Share of participants willing to pay a premium for the more energy efficient product across the different energy label framings.
- Bids placed for products of various energy efficiency levels.

Impact of labels on understanding:

- Share of participants that could correctly identify the most energy efficient product when faced with different energy label framings, with and without prior explanation of label specificities.
- Share of participants that could correctly identify the meaning of specific features of different energy label framings.

Findings

Summarising the findings of both experiments, the authors pinned down a number of elements related to consumer choice when exposed to different energy efficiency labels, as well as to consumer understanding of the labels themselves.

Most importantly, they found evidence that letter-based scales outperformed numerical scales in terms of consumer understanding. The understanding of the A+++ to D scale and of the A to G scale was relatively similar. This translated into letter-based scales leading to higher proportions of consumers opting for energy efficient products with respect to numeric scales. When it came to product choice, the A to G scale seemed to perform better than the A+++ to D scale.

Source

London Economics and IPSOS (2014), *Study on the impact of the energy label and potential changes to it – on consumer understanding and on purchase decisions*, report for the European Commission, Brussels, https://ec.europa.eu/energy/sites/ener/files/documents/Impact%20of%20energy%20labels%20on%20consumer%20behaviour.pdf.

Annex 3.A5

Energy efficiency labelling for online retail – European Commission

Context	
Who?	Study developed by ECORYS, Tilburg University and GfK, ordered by the Consumers, Health, Agriculture and Food Executive Agency (CHAFEA) on behalf of the European Commission.
Where?	10 EU countries (France, Germany, Greece, Ireland, Italy, the Netherlands, Poland, Portugal, Romania, and Sweden)
When?	2014
Why?	The intervention examined how information on energy efficiency labels of household appliances, as well as the timing of its provision, can be improved to promote the choice of more energy efficient products on online retail platforms.
Behavioural intervention	
Environmental policy objective	Promote private investment in more efficient technologies
Behavioural issue	Attitude-behaviour gap; status-quo bias; myopic preferences. A relatively small number of purchases of energy efficient appliances underline a discrepancy between consumers' stated intentions to reduce expenditures on energy and their behaviour at the moment of purchase, where energy efficiency is only one among various product attributes under scrutiny.
Behavioural lever	Simplification and framing of information

Evaluation of the intervention: methodology

Relevant population: Internet users in France, Germany, Greece, Ireland, Italy, the Netherlands, Poland, Portugal, Romania, and Sweden.

Sample size and sampling method(s): The study was conducted online among 11 764 consumers in 10 countries. Countries were selected so as to have a balanced picture of EU member states in terms of internet access, as well as in terms of other characteristics which may affect purchases of durables, such as economic growth rates.

Participants were chosen from GfK's online panels, ensuring nationally representative samples of active internet users.

Method: Stated choice experiment in a simulated online environment testing the effectiveness of four designs of the energy efficiency label. The experiment was followed by a questionnaire surveying experiment participants about their background (socio-demographics, purchasing behaviour) and investigating possible sources of variation in responses to energy efficiency information.

Participants went through the simulation of a shopping trip in an online retail environment selling four different appliances (refrigerators, televisions, washing machines, light bulbs) and were randomly assigned to one of the following two experiments:

- *Consideration experiment*: participants were asked to form a consideration set out of several product alternatives.
  - *Treatments*: the four labels pictured in Figure 3.A5.1.
  - *Control*: no information on energy efficiency.
- *Choice experiment*: participants were asked to make a final product decision out of a restricted set of product alternatives.
  - *Treatments*: the four labels pictured in Figure 3.A5.1; the full EU energy label.
  - *Control*: non-prominent information on energy efficiency, written in the same font as other product attributes.

Figure 3.A5.1. **Reduced label variants tested in the study**

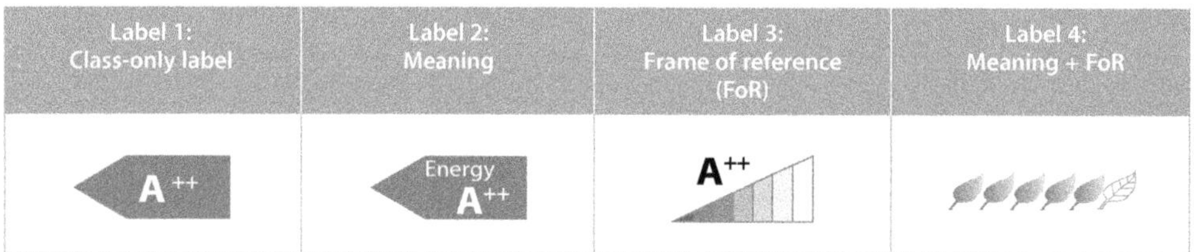

Note: "Energy" is written in the language of the specific country.

Source: ECORYS, Tilburg University and GfK (2014). © European Union, 2014. Reproduction is authorised provided the source is acknowledged.

Within each experiment, the study used a between-subject design, in that energy information shown to participants was varied between subjects.

Units of measurement

Multiple criteria were used to assess the relative effectiveness of different label designs in prompting the consideration/choice of energy efficient goods, e.g.:

- Average energy efficiency level of goods selected in the consideration experiment/ of the good chosen in the choice experiment;
- Probability that the most energy efficient good is selected in the consideration experiment/chosen in the choice experiment.

Findings

- In both experiments, all proposed simplified labels were found to lead to a higher consideration of more energy efficient products than the information provided to the control groups.
- Among simplified labels, the best performing one – all goods considered together – was label 3, which included a frame of reference.
  - Consideration experiment: label 3 led to the most efficient product being included in the consideration set on average 61% of the times as opposed to 51% of the times in the control group (exposed to no information). Label 4 was found

to be the least effective in increasing consideration of more energy efficient products, but still delivered better results than the no information scenario. These results are largely consistent across product categories and across countries (label 3 is the best option in 6 out of 10 countries and is the second-best option in the remaining 4).

- Choice experiment: label 3 led to the most efficient product being selected 68% of the time as opposed to 65% of the time in the control group (exposed to non-prominent information). While differences in impacts among labels were smaller at this stage, all four simplified labels outperformed the standard EU energy label normally shown in physical stores.

Source

ECORYS, Tilburg University and GfK (2014), *Study on the effects on consumer behaviour of online sustainability information displays*, report for the European Commission, Brussels, http://ec.europa.eu/newsroom/dae/document.cfm?doc_id=6151.

Annex 3.A6

Reducing the "hassle factor" – UK

	Context
Who?	Behavioural Insights Team and Department of Energy and Climate Change, in partnership with home improvement retailer B&Q, three Local Authorities in South London (Kingston, Merton and Sutton) and the Global Sustainability Institute (GSI) at Anglia Ruskin University.
Where?	South London, UK.
When?	April – July 2012
Why?	This intervention investigated whether facilitating the preparatory tasks for the installation of loft insulation could increase its uptake. More specifically, it examined whether providing a bundle offering loft clearance together with loft insulation eventually lead more consumers to actually invest in insulating their lofts.
	Behavioural intervention
Environmental policy objective	Promote private investment in more efficient technologies.
Behavioural issue	Attitude-behaviour gap; status-quo bias; myopic preferences. Consumers aim for energy savings but they are reluctant to invest in energy efficiency improvements (e.g. installation of loft insulation) in the short term.
Behavioural lever	Changes to the default policy

Evaluation of the intervention: methodology

Relevant population: Residents of individual houses without loft insulation in the South London area.

Sample size and sampling method(s): 72 480 households, resident in three boroughs in the South London area (Merton, Sutton, Kingston).

The sample was designed to ensure that only appropriate offer-recipient households would be targeted, e.g. excluding areas with a high proportion of flats or rented accommodation or households eligible for free loft insulation schemes.

First, statistical areas were randomly assigned to each of the treatment and control groups. Next, a screening was performed, comparing the profiles of selected statistical areas across groups, in order to ensure treated and control households are similar.

Method: field experiment, designed as a between-group randomised controlled trial.

Loft clearing is viewed as a hassle preventing consumers from undergoing loft insulation. Proposing a bundle including loft clearing in conjunction with loft insulation aims at removing the hassle factor associated with the latter (i.e. clearing out one's loft prior to the insulation works) and thus encouraging energy efficiency investment.

This intervention was based on a change in the default policy: instead of promoting loft insulation by itself, it promoted a bundle including loft clearance and loft insulation services.

72 480 households were contacted by mail with leaflets reporting three different kinds of offers:

- Merton: loft insulation and loft clearance at a cost of GBP 369.
- Sutton: loft insulation and loft clearance at a cost of GBP 450.
- Kingston (control group): standard loft insulation package at a cost of GBP 179.

Interested households were required to contact home improvement retailer B&Q. Follow-up interviews/questionnaires were conducted with households which eventually completed the loft clearance and insulation installation process and with households that did not complete the installation in spite of showing initial interest for it.

Units of measurement: Percentage of households taking up loft insulation following subsidised loft clearance.

Findings

Following the dispatch of the 72 480 leaflets:

- 36 households (0.05%) showed interest in the offer and received audits: very low response to leaflets to perform robust analysis of the differences across groups.
- 28 households (0.04%) installed loft insulation: of these, 25 were in treated groups (Merton and Sutton).

The number of households investing in insulation was too small to perform empirical analysis.

Source

Department of Energy and Climate Change (2013), *Removing the hassle factor associated with loft insulation : Results of a behavioural trial*, DECC, London, https://www.gov.uk/government/uploads/system/uploads/attachment_data/file/236858/DECC_loft_clearance_trial_report_final.pdf.

Annex 3.A7

Individual behaviour in purchasing electric appliances: the energy efficiency fallacy – Switzerland

Detection of an energy efficiency fallacy

Context	
Who?	Swiss Federal Office of Energy, study developed by researchers at ETH Zürich.
Where?	Switzerland
When?	Not specified
Why?	This online experiment was part of a broader behavioural study which investigated consumers' information search behaviour in the context of energy consumption, zooming on the influence that energy-related information has on product choice and energy consumption. In particular, this stated choice experiment investigated the extent to which consumers considered information on energy consumption of appliances on top of their energy efficiency rating when contemplating their purchase.
Behavioural intervention	
Environmental policy objective	Promote private investment in more efficient technologies
Behavioural issue	Attitude-behaviour gap; status-quo bias; myopic preferences. A relatively small number of purchases of energy efficient appliances underline a discrepancy between consumers' stated intentions to reduce expenditures on energy and their behaviour at the moment of purchase, where energy efficiency is only one among various product attributes under scrutiny.
Behavioural lever	Simplification and framing of information

Evaluation of the intervention: methodology

Relevant population: Potential buyers of home appliances in Switzerland.

Sample size and sampling method(s): n = 166, selected from an online panel of 300 individuals.

Respondents participated in three experiments related to energy issues.

Method: Online stated choice experiment with between-subjects design.

Different energy labels for a television with a screen size of 47 inches were designed, yielding four experimental conditions:

a. television with high energy efficiency (A) and high energy consumption (118/kWh/year, based on daily use of 4 hours),

b. television with high energy efficiency (A) and low energy consumption (72/kWh/year),

c. television with low energy efficiency (B) and high energy consumption (118/kWh/year),

d. television with low energy efficiency (B) and low energy consumption (72/kWh/year).

Participants were then randomly assigned to one of these four experimental conditions. After seeing a picture of a television with one such label, they had to indicate the rating of electricity consumption associated with the appliance (between a numerical scale from 0, very low, to 100, very high).

Units of measurement: indication of estimated energy consumption of a given appliance, on a scale from 0 to 100.

Findings

Within the same level of energy consumption (e.g. high or low consumption indicated in the label), participants always estimated lower electricity consumption for A-rated than for B-rated goods. This effect was shown to be statistically significant. As put by the authors, "This means people judged the electricity consumption of a television based on the efficiency class despite differences in actual electricity consumption (kWh). Thus, a television with a good efficiency rating (i.e. A) is automatically associated with low energy consumption, and a television with a worse efficiency rating (i.e. B) is perceived as a product that consumes a lot of energy. This effect will henceforth be termed the energy efficiency fallacy." (Wächter, Sütterlin and Siegrist, 2015a, p. 197)

Source

Wächter, S. M., B. Sütterlin and M. Siegrist (2016), *Investigating energy-friendly consumer behavior. The role of labels, information, and decision-making strategies in the context of energy consumption*, report for the Swiss Federal Office of Energy, Bern, www.bfe.admin.ch/forschungewg/02544/02807/index.html?lang=en&dossier_id=06619.

Wächter, S., B. Sütterlin and M. Siegrist (2015a), "The misleading effect of energy efficiency information on perceived energy friendliness of electric goods", *Journal of Cleaner Production*, 93, 193–202, https://doi.org/10.1016/j.jclepro.2015.01.011.

The energy efficiency fallacy in a comparative setting

	Context
Who?	Swiss Federal Office of Energy, study developed by researchers at ETH Zürich.
Where?	Switzerland
When?	Data were collected from June 3 to June 7, 2013.
Why?	This online stated choice experiment was part of a broader behavioural study which investigated consumers' information search behaviour in the context of energy consumption, zooming on the influence that energy-related information has on product choice and energy consumption. The experiment investigated whether the energy efficiency fallacy emerges in contexts where consumers are exposed to two products at the same time, therefore having the possibility to compare them and their energy labels.
	Behavioural intervention
Environmental policy objective	Promote private investment in more efficient technologies
Behavioural issue	Attitude-behaviour gap; myopic preferences. A relatively small number of purchases of energy efficient appliances underline a discrepancy between consumers' stated intentions to reduce expenditures on energy and their behaviour at the moment of purchase, where energy efficiency is only one among various product attributes under scrutiny.
Behavioural lever	Simplification and framing of information

Evaluation of the intervention: methodology

Relevant population: Potential buyers of home appliances in Switzerland.

Sample size and sampling method(s): n = 305. Participants were recruited from an online panel of 330 users provided by a market research institute. They received a small incentive for their participation (about EUR 2.5).

Method: stated choice experiment with between-subjects design.

All participants were exposed to the same tasks and questions; the only variation was the order with which the products were portrayed in the tasks, which was randomised.

Consumers were shown the descriptions of a couple of products belonging to the same class, side by side: first two televisions, then two freezers.

The product descriptions contained information which is routinely present on in-store labels: energy labels and technical specifications (e.g. display technology for televisions, volume for freezers).

The two televisions and the two freezers differed in their energy efficiency class, in size and in annual electricity consumption: the larger television/freezer was characterised by a high energy efficiency rating and high annual energy consumption, whereas the small counterpart for both products was characterised by a lower energy efficiency rating and more modest annual energy consumption.

Participants were asked to pick one of the two televisions/freezers as if they had to recommend it to a highly energy-conscious person. The choice decision was not framed as choice for personal use in order to prevent participants from choosing a product on the basis of personal preferences regarding technical specificities other than energy efficiency (e.g. screen size for televisions).

Units of measurement: Share of participants recommending a given appliance.

Findings

As table 3.A7.1 shows, 45% of participants recommended the television with high annual electricity consumption. When it came to freezers, the high annual energy consumption appliance was recommended by 73% of participants. The authors explain these results as follows:

"Results suggest that a majority of the participants based their decision on the energy efficiency information. The difference in the percentages for the TV and freezer tasks might be due to the different emotional attachment to these products. A television fulfils various functions (e.g. status symbol, symbol of affinity for technology of its owner) in addition to its actual purpose (i.e. transmitting moving images) whereas a freezer keeps its actual purpose as a cooling unit. People might spend more time on and evaluate more information for a product they are emotionally attached to, which can explain the higher number of correct answers in the television task". (Wächter, Sütterlin and Siegrist, 2015a, p. 198)

Table 3.A7.1. **Distribution of participants' product recommendations for an energy-conscious person**

	High annual electricity consumption, high energy efficiency	**Low annual electricity consumption, low energy efficiency**
Television	45%	55%
Freezer	73%	27%

Source: adapted from (Wächter, Sütterlin and Siegrist, 2015a).

Source

Wächter, S. M., B. Sütterlin and M. Siegrist (2016), *Investigating energy-friendly consumer behavior. The role of labels, information, and decision-making strategies in the context of energy consumption*, report for the Swiss Federal Office of Energy, Bern, www.bfe.admin.ch/forschungewg/02544/02807/index.html?lang=en&dossier_id=06619.

Wächter, S., B. Sütterlin and M. Siegrist (2015a), "The misleading effect of energy efficiency information on perceived energy friendliness of electric goods", *Journal of Cleaner Production*, 93, 193–202, https://doi.org/10.1016/j.jclepro.2015.01.011.

Confusing appliances' energy efficiency ratings and energy consumption

Context	
Who?	Swiss Federal Office of Energy, study developed by researchers at ETH Zürich.
Where?	Switzerland
When?	Not specified
Why?	This online stated choice experiment was part of a broader behavioural study which investigated consumers' information search behaviour in the context of energy consumption, zooming on the influence that energy-related information has on product choice and energy consumption. This experiment studied the perception of energy friendliness that consumers have when comparing electric appliances belonging to different product categories along both their energy efficiency rating (e.g. A+++ to D as in the EU energy label) and their annual energy consumption (kWh/year). Product categories were chosen in order to have a good traditionally associated with high energy consumption (e.g. freezers) and one associated with lower energy consumption (e.g. refrigerators).
Behavioural intervention	
Environmental policy objective	Promote private investment in more efficient technologies
Behavioural issue	Attitude-behaviour gap; myopic preferences. A relatively small number of purchases of energy efficient appliances underline a discrepancy between consumers' stated intentions to reduce expenditures on energy and their behaviour at the moment of purchase, where energy efficiency is only one among various product attributes under scrutiny.
Behavioural lever	Simplification and framing of information

Evaluation of the intervention: methodology

Relevant population: Potential buyers of home appliances in Switzerland.

Sample size and sampling method(s): n = 166, selected from an online panel of 300 individuals.

Respondents participated in three experiments related to energy issues.

Method: online stated choice experiment.

Participants were randomly assigned to the control group or to one of two experimental treatments.

Participants of all groups were simultaneously shown pictures of a freezer and a fridge, with their corresponding energy efficiency labels.

In the control group, the two products virtually had the same level of annual energy consumption and the same energy efficiency rating.

In the treatment groups, the energy efficiency rating and annual energy consumption of the refrigerator shown in the labels was *the same* under both treatments. When it came to the freezer, however, while annual energy consumption was the same under both treatments and always *higher* than that of the refrigerator, the energy efficiency rating varied as follows:

- Treatment **(a)**: freezer and refrigerator had the same energy efficiency rating.
- Treatment **(b)**: the freezer's energy efficiency rating was lower than that of the refrigerator.

Units of measurement: indication of estimated energy consumption prompted by the question "How much electricity does the freezer consume compared to the refrigerator?"

Participants had to indicate their answer on a scale from 0 (the freezer consumes much less than the refrigerator) to 100 (the freezer consumes much more than the refrigerator), where 50 indicated equal consumption for the two appliances.

Findings

As explained by the authors, "Hypothesizing that the energy efficiency class determines how the electricity consumption of a freezer in relation to a refrigerator is perceived, the following results were expected: The electricity consumption in condition (a) (high efficiency) should be rated lower compared with condition (b) (low efficiency) as we expected the participants to mainly consider the energy efficiency class for their estimation. Thus, in condition (a), the estimate of the electricity consumption of the freezer relative to the fridge should approach the level of the refrigerator." (Wächter, Sütterlin and Siegrist, 2015a, p. 199)

Participants estimated the freezer's energy consumption to be substantially higher than the refrigerator's under treatment (b) than under treatment (a), even though in both treatment conditions the freezer's label reported an annual energy consumption of 201 kWh/year. More specifically, under treatment (b) the estimated energy consumption of the freezer relative to the refrigerator was 77 (on a scale from 0 to 100, as indicated above), whereas this figure was 67.2 under treatment (a). This difference was statistically significant ($p = 0.02$).

The authors explain this stating that "the energy efficiency fallacy might distort the perceived electricity consumption (i.e. energy friendliness) of a product category that generally consumes an excessive amount of energy. This finding strengthens the hypothesis that the energy efficiency class is used as the basis for judgments, although participants could have compared the information on actual electricity consumption (kWh/year)" (Wächter, Sütterlin and Siegrist, 2015a, p. 200).

The fallacy led participants to think that the freezer consumed as much as the refrigerator just because they both had a high energy efficiency rating, ignoring information on annual electricity consumption.

Source

Wächter, S. M., B. Sütterlin and M. Siegrist (2016), *Investigating energy-friendly consumer behavior. The role of labels, information, and decision-making strategies in the context of energy consumption*, report for the Swiss Federal Office of Energy, Bern, www.bfe.admin.ch/forschungewg/02544/02807/index.html?lang=en&dossier_id=06619.

Wächter, S., B. Sütterlin and M. Siegrist (2015a), "The misleading effect of energy efficiency information on perceived energy friendliness of electric goods", *Journal of Cleaner Production*, 93, 193–202, https://doi.org/10.1016/j.jclepro.2015.01.011.

Understanding consumer perception of energy labels with eye-tracking

Context	
Who?	Swiss Federal Office of Energy, study developed by researchers at ETH Zürich.
Where?	Switzerland
When?	Not specified
Why?	This eye-tracking experiment is part of a broader behavioural study which investigated consumers' information search behaviour in the context of energy consumption, zooming on the influence that energy-related information has on product choice and on energy consumption. This specific experiment aims at understanding consumers' reactions to the EU energy label by using eye-tracking methodology.
Behavioural intervention	
Environmental policy objective	Promote private investment in more efficient technologies
Behavioural issue	Attitude-behaviour gap; myopic preferences. A relatively small number of purchases of energy efficient appliances underline a discrepancy between consumers' stated intentions to reduce expenditures on energy and their behaviour at the moment of purchase, where energy efficiency is only one among various product attributes under scrutiny.
Behavioural lever	Simplification and framing of information

Evaluation of the intervention: methodology

Relevant population: Potential buyers of home appliances in German-speaking areas of Switzerland.

Sample size and sampling method(s): n = 117, the subsample of eligible individuals who agreed to participate starting from a random sample of 500 German-speaking households to whom an invitation letter was sent. Individuals under 20 and over 65 years old, as well as those wearing glasses or hard contact lenses, or suffering from eye diseases were excluded due to technical requirements of eye-tracking machinery.

Participants received a small sum of money as an incentive to take part in the experiment.

Method: lab (eye-tracking) experiment with between-subject design.

Two sets of products were shown to participants in randomised sequence: freezers and televisions.

Participants had to pick a product out of four options being given information on, *inter alia*, their price, energy efficiency, volume (freezers), screen size (televisions). The menu of options was representative of what could be on sale in an online shop. The product whose label was indicating the highest level of energy efficiency was not necessarily the one with the lowest annual energy consumption.

Participants were randomly exposed to one of four experimental conditions:

1. choosing a product for oneself, with information in a table format (without energy labels);
2. choosing a product for oneself, with information in a table format and the corresponding energy labels;
3. choosing a product for a person who would want to save energy, with information in a table format (without energy labels); and
4. choosing a product for a person who would want to save energy, with information in a table format and the corresponding energy labels.

The eye tracker monitored fixation over the various "areas of interest" present in the material presented to participants. Fixation, which is measured when the eye remains still for a given period of time, indicates underlying cognitive processes and attention to a given element.

Units of measurement

The following parameters related to fixation were monitored:

- Dwell time or gaze duration.
- Number of fixations.
- Mean fixation duration: fixation time divided by the fixation count.

Findings

The experiment showed that exposing participants to the energy label increased their focus on energy-related information (energy consumption and energy efficiency rating), especially in conditions 4, where participants were to pay special attention to energy savings. Energy efficiency ratings appeared to be processed by participants in a shorter time if reported through labels. However, that was the case only when choosing among televisions; not when choosing among freezers. Furthermore, in spite of increased focus, labels did not appear to necessarily increase energy-friendly choices.

Ultimately, the findings are rather mixed, as in the authors' words "[t]he study's results partially support the EU's mandatory policy, showing that the energy label triggers attention toward energy information in general. However, the energy label's effect on consumers' actual product choices seems to be rather low. The study's results show that the currently used presentation format on the label is insufficient. The findings suggest that it does not facilitate the integration of energy-related information. Furthermore, the current format can attract consumers to focus more on energy-efficiency information, leading them to disregard information about actual energy consumption. As a result, the final energy consumption may increase because excellent ratings on energy efficiency (e.g. A++) do not automatically imply little consumption" (Wächter, Sütterlin and Siegrist, 2015b, p. 1).

Source

Wächter, S. M., B. Sütterlin and M. Siegrist (2016), *Investigating energy-friendly consumer behavior. The role of labels, information, and decision-making strategies in the context of energy consumption*, report for the Swiss Federal Office of Energy, Bern, www.bfe.admin.ch/forschungewg/02544/02807/index.html?lang=en&dossier_id=06619.

Wächter, S. M., B. Sütterlin and M. Siegrist (2015b), "Desired and undesired effects of energy labels – An eye-tracking study", PLoS ONE, 10(7), 1–26. https://doi.org/10.1371/journal.pone.0134132.

Annex 3.A8

Defaults in green electricity markets – Switzerland

Context	
Who?	Swiss Federal Office of Energy, study developed by researchers at ETH Zürich.
Where?	The experiment was run at the ETH Decision Science Laboratory in Zurich, Switzerland.
When?	June-September 2015
Why?	This lab experiment tested what type of electricity source mix consumers ultimately choose when exposed to different types of electricity contracts.
Behavioural intervention	
Environmental policy objective	Incentivise environmentally sustainable consumption patterns
Behavioural issue	The choice of electricity contracts is characterised by status-quo bias. This may prevent "green" consumers, burdened by inertia, from shifting to an electricity contract offering the energy mix better matching their preferences (e.g. 100% renewable energy).
Behavioural lever	Changes to the default policy

Evaluation of the intervention: methodology

Relevant population: Households in Switzerland.

Sample size and sampling method(s): n = 161. All participants were university students, largely undergraduate; therefore the majority of them had no experience with the choice of electricity contracts.

Method: lab experiment.

Participants were given a fixed budget and had to choose their preferred electricity mix for a given amount of kWh, between green and conventional electricity. While conventional electricity was always cheaper than green electricity, the price of the latter changed across five choice scenarios, according to the renewable source used to generate it (e.g. hydro or solar power), in order to mimic real world prices.

More specifically, the five choice situations differed in the price premium that green electricity bore relative to conventional electricity: a premium of CHF 0.01, CHF 0.03, CHF 0.1, CHF 0.15 or CHF 0.2 per kWh of green electricity.

Participants were randomly allocated to one of three treatments:

1. *Active choice*: participants actively selected their preferred mix of green/conventional electricity.
2. *Green electricity default*: participants received green electricity as their default power supply. In this treatment condition, participants could either stick to the default option, or opt out of it and choose their preferred energy mix.

3. *Grey electricity default*: participants received conventional ("grey") electricity as their default power supply. On top of this and of the normal budget, they received additional budget to replace conventional electricity with green electricity. Again, participants could either stick to the default option, or opt out of it and choose their preferred energy mix.

When exposed to green or grey defaults, participants could move away from the default option by choosing another energy mix between five alternative contract options:

- *Alternatives to grey default option*: 10% green electricity, 40% green electricity, 60% green electricity, 90% green electricity and 100% green electricity.
- *Alternatives to green default option*: 0% green electricity, 10% green electricity, 40% green electricity, 60% green electricity and 90% green electricity.

In both cases, shifting away from the default option required going through different effortful reporting tasks.

Choosing 100% green electricity depleted the whole budget (which varied with the price of renewable energy to allow for this freedom), while choosing a portion of conventional electricity allowed participants to keep a part of it. Participants faced a trade-off between opting for more expensive green energy, contributing to a public good (the reduction in harmful emissions), and cheaper conventional energy, which on the other hand gave them a monetary payoff.

Units of measurement

- Percentage of participants opting for 100% green electricity.
- Mean share of green electricity in electricity contracts.

Findings

When the price premium for green electricity was *low* (up to CHF 0.03 per kWh), green defaults led participants to choose significantly more green electricity than in the active choice and grey default situations. For example, with a price premium of CHF 0.01 per kWh, the mean share of green electricity in contracts reached 86% under a green default, 67% under active choice and 71% under a grey default.

This signals a mismatch between consumer preferences in the active choice and green default case. This is explained by the fact that consumers find that opting out of the green default requires too high a cost – in terms of effort – relatively to the benefit of having an electricity contract closer to their preferences. Thus, as the author puts it, they "overreact" to the green default by keeping more often the contract with the 100% green energy mix. Conversely, the difference in the share of renewable energy between the active choice and grey default case was not statistically significant.

When the price premium for renewable energy was *higher* (between 0.04 and 0.2 CHF per kWh), there was no statistically significant difference between the mean share of green electricity in contracts allowing active choice and those with the green default option. Under that renewable energy price scenario, consumer preferences for green electricity under active choice were matched with those under the green default scenario. It is thus important to offer consumers the opportunity to modulate their energy mix flexibly, as done in this experiment. This choice possibility seems to be preferred to contracts based on an entirely green or entirely grey energy mix.

Source

Ghesla, C. (forthcoming), "Defaults in Green Electricity Markets – Preference Match not Guaranteed", *Journal of the Association of Environmental and Resource Economists.*

Annex 3.A9

Environmental footprint labelling and consumer behaviour – European Commission

Context	
Who?	Ipsos MORI, London Economics and AEA were commissioned this study by the European Commission Directorate-General for Energy.
Where?	9 European countries (UK, France, Germany, Italy, Norway, Poland, Romania, Spain, Estonia)
When?	2012
Why?	The intervention tested two alternative designs for environmental footprint labels, to be possibly added to product energy efficiency labels. The ultimate objective was to: a) assess which of the two designs is likely to encourage the purchase of more environmentally friendly products (washing machines, televisions, light bulbs), and b) understand how much consumers would be willing to pay for products with different environmental footprints.
Behavioural intervention	
Environmental policy objective	Incentivise environmentally sustainable consumption patterns; Promote private investment in more efficient technologies.
Behavioural issue	Attitude-behaviour gap; status-quo bias; myopic preferences.
Behavioural lever	Simplification and framing of information

Evaluation of the intervention: methodology

Relevant population: Households in 9 European countries (UK, France, Germany, Italy, Norway, Poland, Romania, Spain, Estonia).

Sample size and sampling method(s): 6409 participants (United Kingdom: 884 participants; France: 925; Germany: 926; Italy: 898; Norway: 525; Poland: 508; Romania: 502; Spain: 737; Estonia: 504).

"The data from the experiment was weighted back to the known profile of the population in each market (by age, gender and work status) to ensure the findings were nationally representative." (Ipsos MORI, London Economics and AEA, 2012, p. 89).

Method:

The study was developed in three phases: it consisted of: i) a review of existing studies; ii) qualitative discussion groups with consumers to elicit initial reactions to alternative designs of environmental footprint labels; and iii) two behavioural experiments (a bidding experiment and a stated choice experiment, both carried out on an online platform) and a survey.

The experiments aimed at testing how environmental footprint labels could impact consumer preferences and willingness to pay for three categories of products (washing machines, televisions and light bulbs) differing in their environmental footprint. Two alternative designs for environmental footprint labels were tested, to be added alongside energy efficiency labels:

- *Proposed Energy and Environmental Label*: this design added four environmental lifecycle indicators (carbon footprint, water footprint, resource depletion and water eco-toxicity) to the EU energy efficiency label.
- *Proposed Energy and Carbon Footprint Label*: this design added only the lifecycle carbon footprint indicator to the energy efficiency label.

Additionally, participants were exposed to one of the following conditions prior to the start of the experiments:

- *No information group*: no information on the meaning of labels,
- *Explanation group*: explanation of the current EU energy efficiency label, as well as of the two proposed labels including environmental impact information.
- *Explanation plus prompt group*: on top of receiving label explanations, these participants were prompted to consider these elements in their bids and product choices.

Bidding experiment

Participants were shown a product with its label, they were informed of its redemption value (i.e. the amount for which they could redeem a product successfully secured in the experiment) and of the price range of the product. They received a fixed endowment and were invited to place a bid for the product.

If their offer was higher than the product's sale price, respondents "won" it, earning the redemption value net of the sale price. This net value was given to them in the form of shopping vouchers (incentivised experiment).

In order to reward environmentally friendly choices, when respondents "secured" environmentally friendly products, a financial contribution was donated to a fund dedicated to environmental protection.

Consumers were required to place three bids for each of the three products: washing machine, television and light bulb.

They were randomly allocated to one of two groups:

- Group 1 was exposed either to the proposed Energy and Environmental Label or to the standard EU energy efficiency label;
- Group 2 was exposed either to the proposed Energy and Carbon Footprint Label or to the standard EU energy efficiency label.

Choice experiment

Participants were asked to make a hypothetical choice between two alternatives for each product category (washing machines, televisions and light bulbs) differing in their environmental ratings and prices.

They were randomly allocated to one of two groups:

- Group 1 was exposed either to the proposed Energy and Environmental Label or to the standard EU energy efficiency label;
- Group 2 was exposed either to the proposed Energy and Carbon Footprint Label or to the standard EU energy efficiency label.

Units of measurement

- *Bidding experiment*: Willingness to pay for products labelled with the proposed labels.
- *Choice experiment*: Share of consumers choosing the more environmentally friendly product.
- Share of consumers correctly interpreting labels.

Findings

Impact on willingness to pay and purchase decisions:

- Consumers placed higher bids for more environmentally friendly products when they were shown the environmental footprint or the carbon footprint label.
- Both footprint labels encouraged consumers to purchase more environmentally friendly goods, *ceteris paribus*. It did not seem that the composite environmental footprint label changed behaviour to a greater extent than the carbon footprint label.

Understanding of label meanings and its impact on purchase decisions:

- If they had a higher level of understanding of the label, respondents were more likely to choose the better performing product (from a lifecycle analysis perspective) and to be willing to pay more for it. This was shown to be valid for both labels.
- Consumers exposed to explanatory information on the labels had a better understanding of the ratings.

Differences in impacts across products:

- The labels seemed to increase willingness to pay for washing machines and televisions but not for light bulbs, possibly because of the lower monetary stakes associated with purchasing the latter.

Behavioural drivers of label understanding and purchase decisions:

- Consumers are likely to focus mainly on standard indicators such as product performance characteristics and less so on environmental or carbon footprint indicators, especially when their understanding of the latter is limited.
- Consumers' pro-environment stances or prior exposure to product labelling do not seem to strongly drive their willingness to pay for greener products.

Source

Ipsos MORI, London Economics and AEA (2012), *Research on EU product label options*, report for the European Commission, Brussels, https://ec.europa.eu/energy/sites/ener/files/documents/2012-12-research-eu-product-label-options.pdf.

Notes

1. Smart meters record and convey real-time electricity information to electric utilities. Connecting smart meters to salient devices such as in-home displays, real-time information on energy consumption and/or energy prices can be made available to consumers in an intuitive and timely format.

2. The average historical savings from the applications reviewed in the report amount to about 6% per year (for consumers with electric heating and no automation). The authors of the report state that this figure is a realistic estimate of the potential of feedback mechanisms for energy conservation in Norway.

3. As explained in Schubert and Stadelmann (2016), the Swiss government has adopted the EU energy label for household appliances. However, the display of these labels in online retail platforms was not yet fully enforced when the study took place, which is why the baseline situation is one where no energy information was displayed alongside product information.

4. Unlike other laboratory experiments analysed in this report, all participants in this experiment were students.

References

AECOM (2011), *Energy Demand Research Project: Final Analysis*, report for OFGEM.

Allcott, H. (2011), "Social norms and energy conservation", *Journal of Public Economics*, 95(9–10), pp. 1082–1095, http://dx.doi.org/10.1016/j.jpubeco.2011.03.003.

Behavioural Insights Team (2016), *The Behavioural Insights Team Update Report 2015-2016*, Behavioural Insights Ltd., London.

Cabinet Office Behavioural Insights Team, Department of Energy and Climate Change and Department for Communities and Local Government (2011), *Behaviour Change and Energy Use*, London.

Department of Energy and Climate Change (2014a), *Advice on how to use heating controls: Evaluation of a trial in Newcastle*, DECC, London.

Department of Energy and Climate Change (2014b), *Evaluation of the DECC / John Lewis energy labelling trial*, DECC, London.

Department of Energy and Climate Change (2013), *Removing the hassle factor associated with loft insulation : Results of a behavioural trial*, DECC, London.

ECORYS, Tilburg University and GfK (2014), *Study on the effects on consumer behaviour of online sustainability information displays*, report for the European Commission, Brussels, http://dx.doi.org/10.2759/52063.

European Commission (2015), *Proposal for a Regulation of the European Parliament and of the Council setting a framework for energy efficiency labelling and repealing Directive 2010/30/EU*, Brussels.

Ghesla, C. (forthcoming), "Defaults in Green Electricity Markets – Preference Match not Guaranteed", *Journal of the Association of Environmental and Resource Economists*.

Ipsos MORI, London Economics and AEA (2012), *Research on EU product label options*, report for the European Commission, Brussels.

Kallbekken, S., H. Sælen and E. A. Hermansen (2013), "Bridging the energy efficiency gap: A field experiment on lifetime energy costs and household appliances", *Journal of Consumer Policy, 36*(1), 1-16.

London Economics and IPSOS (2014), *Study on the impact of the energy label and potential changes to it – on consumer understanding and on purchase decisions*, report for the European Commission, Brussels.

Norwegian Water Resources and Energy Directorate (2014), *Smarte målere (AMS) og feedback (Assessing the potential of energy consumption feedback in Norway)*, Oslo.

Schubert, R. and M. Stadelmann (2016), *Energy-Using Durables : Driving Forces of Purchase Decisions*, report for the Swiss Federal Office of Energy, Bern.

Social and Behavioral Sciences Team (2016), *Social and Behavioral Sciences Team 2016 Annual Report*, Office of Science and Technology Policy, Washington, DC.

Wächter, S. M., B. Sütterlin and M. Siegrist (2016), *Investigating energy-friendly consumer behavior. The role of labels, information, and decision-making strategies in the context of energy consumption*, report for the Swiss Federal Office of Energy, Bern.

Wächter, S. M., B. Sütterlin and M. Siegrist (2015a), "The misleading effect of energy efficiency information on perceived energy friendliness of electric goods", *Journal of Cleaner Production, 93*, 193–202, http://doi.org/10.1016/j.jclepro.2015.01.011.

Wächter, S. M., B. Sütterlin and M. Siegrist (2015b), "Desired and undesired effects of energy labels – An eye-tracking study", *PLoS ONE, 10*(7), 1–26, http://doi.org/10.1371/journal.pone.0134132.

Chapter 4

Using behavioural insights to promote more sustainable transport choices

This chapter analyses behavioural interventions implemented to induce consumers to make more sustainable transport and car choices. The behavioural biases at play are highlighted, together with the behavioural levers used by policy makers to tackle them. Behavioural interventions in this area have focused on framing information on cars' fuel efficiency, emissions and running costs in a clear and salient way.

The statistical data for Israel are supplied by and under the responsibility of the relevant Israeli authorities. The use of such data by the OECD is without prejudice to the status of the Golan Heights, East Jerusalem and Israeli settlements in the West Bank under the terms of international law.

Unlike in the energy consumption case, the connection between fuel consumption and service obtained (e.g. powering a motorised vehicle) is quite salient in the transport sector. This is due to the clear price-quantity match observed as consumers refuel their vehicles, and to the visible fuel meter in vehicles themselves. However, in the transport realm, three types of behaviour are prone to behavioural biases (see Reader's Guide for definitions of all technical terms):

First, *fuel consumption* in motorised transport is associated with driving routines and habits. Framing and social norms can help in turning such habits into a "greener", more fuel efficient, driving style. Framing can clarify and make more salient the connection between specific driving patterns and fuel consumption. Social norms could play a role as a behavioural lever by providing individuals feedback on their driving behaviour relative to other fellow owners of same-sized vehicles.

Second, the *purchase of a motor vehicle* is – like the purchase of any other durable good – an infrequent event from the household's perspective. Hence, it is subject to all the biases characterising investments in energy efficiency improvements such as myopia and inertia induced by perceptions of sunk costs.

Furthermore, as cars can also serve the purpose of status symbols (Kahn, 2007), car choice is more exposed to the influence of social norms. Indeed, *fuel efficiency* does not always rank high among the attributes considered in the purchase of motor vehicles. For this reason, increasing its salience, especially at the moment of purchase, may be crucial to ensure that consumers take it into account in the choice process.

Third, *choice among transport modes* (e.g. public transport, motor vehicles, non-motorised modes, such as bicycles) is subject to inertia and social norms. Individuals may stick to car commuting because of inertia, even though they may have to incur substantially higher financial costs (e.g. fuel, car maintenance, insurance) and time costs (due to congestion) in comparison with commuting with other modes.

Framing the private and social costs of car commuting (e.g. contribution to congestion and air pollution; aggregate number of hours spent driving per year; use of public space for street-side parking) in order to make them more salient may help individuals reconsider their routine commuting choices and patterns by weighing their costs and benefits.

Framing of fuel efficiency, emissions and running costs information

When it comes to car purchases, consumers often show attitude-behaviour gaps. While being aware of the environmental impact of cars and stating that they see fuel economy as an important criterion for car choice, these attitudes do not ultimately translate into eco-friendly car purchases. This may also be due to a lack of understanding of the link between a vehicle's fuel efficiency class and the environmental impact of its use.

To better understand their weight on car purchase decisions, in 2013 the *European Commission* ordered an impact assessment of different types of labels and promotional materials providing information on fuel efficiency, CO_2 emissions and running costs (Codagnone, Bogliacino and Veltri, 2013 – see Annex 4.A1). The study built on a three-fold approach consisting of a cross-country survey, a stated choice experiment rolled out on an online platform (both carried out in 10 EU member states), and a laboratory experiment (carried out in the UK). In the lab, analysts focused on testing alternative designs for environmental impact labels. In the online choice experiment, they also tested different designs for promotional material. The effectiveness of the different treatments (labels and promotional materials) was measured through various indicators:

- *Willingness to pay*: does the information embedded in labels/promotional material drive consumers to spend more for eco-friendly and/or fuel efficient cars or in spending less for eco unfriendly and/or fuel inefficient ones?
- *Self-reported and constructed cognitive measures of the noticeability, comprehension and recall of relevant information*: consumers were asked questions on car "greenness" and fuel efficiency. Their answers were used to infer how noticeable and comprehensible information was in labels and promotional material.

Among the most conclusive findings of the experiments, there were two main points. First, labels drawing on fuel economy indicators (e.g. information on foregone fuel savings, fuel costs presented in different formats) were more effective than those drawing on emission-related indicators. Second, the most effective promotional materials (stand-alone leaflets) included the graphic illustration of CO_2 emissions and the use of larger elements indicating running costs per 5 years. In general, interventions involving fuel costs (both in the per mile/km format and in the per 5 years format) were shown to be the most effective among all the tested ones.

While the European Commission's project tested the impact of salient information provision on consumer understanding and willingness to pay for fuel efficient cars, in June 2015 the *Israeli Ministry of Environmental Protection* ran a stated choice experiment to test the impact of alternative fuel efficiency labels on car choice (see Annex 4.A2). The experiment was run by the Ministry's unit dedicated to the design and implementation of behavioural interventions. More specifically, the experiment tested the extent to which different types of fuel efficiency labels induce consumers to purchase more fuel efficient cars.

Consumers were asked to make a car purchase decision in a simulated retail environment. In this setting, they were shown 7 pairs of cars, with each pair differing in price, fuel consumption and pollution emissions. In each pair, one car was more expensive but also more efficient, to the extent that this option would represent a better economic choice in the long run. Consumers in the control group were shown solely the price tag and the standard fuel efficiency label, including information on fuel consumption per 100 km and pollutant emissions.[1] All the other consumers were exposed to different combinations of the following additional pieces of information according to the treatment group they were assigned to:

- the tax benefit that the car owner could be granted upon purchase of a car of a certain fuel efficiency class;
- the estimated fuel costs for a period of 5 years;
- a comparison of fuel consumption and costs with respect to the best-in-class (most fuel efficient) or the average car of the same category.

The label comparing long-term fuel costs to those required by the best-in-class car in the same category was found to be more effective in inducing consumers to opt for more fuel efficient car models than the standard label. More precisely, about 77% of consumers exposed to this label opted for the more efficient car in the pair, compared to about 71% in the control group. This was likely due to the impact of loss aversion: such comparison effectively underlined the financial costs of driving a car that is less fuel efficient than a given benchmark.

While these findings have not yet prompted changes in fuel efficiency labels in Europe and in Israel, scientific evidence on the advantages of making fuel costs more salient has informed concrete policy change in the *United States*. Traditionally, car fuel efficiency figures in the United States have been expressed in miles per gallon. However, Larrick and Soll (2008) showed that the non-linearity of this indicator makes its interpretation difficult for consumers, who ultimately may fail to grasp its meaning and thus choose less energy efficient vehicles.

Taking stock of scientific evidence, in 2011 the US Environmental Protection Agency updated the regulations regarding fuel efficiency labels. The new labels are required to depict vehicles' fuel efficiency with two linear measures: gallons per 100 miles and estimated annual fuel costs. This is an example of behaviourally informed policy. It remains to be assessed whether car labels including two alternative indicators for the same concept are clearly understood by consumers.

Conclusion on transport choices

In the field of transport, the applications of behavioural insights reviewed in this report have thus far revolved around simplifying and framing information, in order to increase the effectiveness of fuel efficiency labels and their role in car choice.

While not numerous, stated choice experiments have been a common methodology in the transport-related behavioural interventions reviewed in this report (2 interventions). The reason why this may be the case is that such experiments are particularly convenient for the simulation of purchase decisions on online shopping platforms, which provide an information mine for consumers prior to making their final choice at car dealers' shops.

The main results from behavioural interventions in this field show that translating fuel efficiency indicators into expected fuel costs throughout a period of multiple years can be highly effective in driving consumers towards the purchase of more fuel efficient vehicles, as the experiment developed in Israel has shown. This finding mirrors similar evidence from the energy efficiency sector: just as pointing out energy costs for the use of domestic appliances can make the value of investing in energy efficient ones apparent, making running costs of cars more salient will induce consumers to assign a higher weight to fuel efficiency at the moment of car choice.

This insight has already driven policy change in at least one case: a concrete behaviourally motivated policy change has been implemented in the United States. In 2011, the US EPA mandated a change in the framing of fuel efficiency labels to include information on the fuel costs associated with car use.[2]

Another policy-relevant result from these interventions is that indicators of pollution and CO_2 emissions from car use are too complex for synthetic labelling. They are better understood by consumers when explained in a more detailed and salient way in elaborate promotional materials such as stand-alone leaflets. This result points to the need to further develop tools to convey information about the pollution externalities from the use of motor vehicles (Codagnone, Bogliacino and Veltri, 2013).

Behavioural insights could also contribute to policies aimed at shifting the choice among transport modes towards more sustainable options (e.g. biking, public transport): this is an area in which the potential of behavioural insights is still largely underexploited.

Annex 4.A1

Testing CO_2/Car labelling options and consumer information – European Commission

	Context
Who?	Study realised by Cristiano Codagnone (Università degli Studi di Milano and Universitat Oberta de Catalunya), Francesco Bogliacino (Fundación Universitaria Konrad Lorenz) and Giuseppe Veltri (University of East Anglia) on behalf of the European Commission (DG Clima).
Where?	10 EU countries (Belgium, Germany, France, Italy, Netherlands, Poland, Romania, Spain, Sweden, United Kingdom).
When?	2013
Why?	The objective of this intervention was to test with an experimental approach: • the effectiveness of variants of car eco-labels, both related to their content and to their layout; • the effectiveness of mandatory information on fuel efficiency and CO_2 emissions in promotional material.
	Behavioural intervention
Environmental policy objective	Promote private investment in more efficient technologies
Behavioural issue	Lack of understanding of indicators of environmental impact and fuel efficiency of cars. Attitude-behaviour gaps: consumers may be aware of the environmental impact of cars – e.g. air pollution, greenhouse gas emissions – but this may not necessarily translate into the purchase of more fuel efficient and environmentally friendly cars. This is also due to myopia in intertemporal choices.
Behavioural lever	Simplification and framing of information

Evaluation of the intervention: methodology

Relevant population: Perspective car buyers in the EU.

Sample size and sampling method(s)

- ***Preparatory phase (preliminary survey)***: N = 8000 respondents (representative random sample of 800 respondents from each of the following 10 countries: Belgium, Germany, France, Italy, Netherlands, Poland, Romania, Spain, Sweden, United Kingdom).
- ***Laboratory experiment***: N = 405 respondents recruited by the London School of Economics (LSE) Behavioural Lab from a panel of respondents; not representative of the general population.
- ***Online choice experiment***: same sample as in the preparatory phase.

Method

The study included 4 phases:

1. **Preparatory phase**: review of the literature and preliminary survey in 10 countries. The objective of this phase was to understand:
   a. What parameters affect the car-purchase process (e.g. price, fuel efficiency, self-reported attitudes)?
   b. What is the level of consumers' awareness regarding the environmental impact of car usage, both in absolute and relative terms (e.g. environmental impact of a car relative to similar cars)?
2. **Laboratory experiment** testing the effectiveness of labels and promotional materials.
3. **Stated choice experiment** in a simulated online environment, re-testing labels' effectiveness (as in the lab experiment) and testing promotional material.
4. **Analysis and recommendations**: econometric and multivariate statistical analysis aimed at deriving policy implications and recommendations.

Both the laboratory experiment and the stated choice experiment were designed as randomised controlled trials with between-subjects design: participants were randomly allocated to a treatment or to a control group (placebo). In the lab experiment, the control condition was the car label in use in the UK, since the experiment was run in London.

The treatments tested in the lab and the simulated online environment involved variations on the content and layout of labels and promotional material for cars (conventional, electric and hybrid cars):

- *Labels*: the trial tested both standard elements normally found in car labels (e.g. CO_2 classification systems, in absolute terms or relative to a car belonging to the same class) and additional elements (e.g. information about fuel costs in per mile/km format and in per 5 years format, carbon taxation, savings relative to fuel efficient benchmarks). These treatments have been tested both in the lab and in the online experiment.
- *Promotional material*: general layout, additional elements (e.g. combinations of CO_2 emissions indicators with information on fuel costs) and presence of weblinks. These treatments have been tested in the online experiment.

The authors of the study used regression analysis to estimate the difference in means between treated groups and control groups with respect to the response variable used (see below, *Units of measurement*): this pins down the causal effect of the treatment considered.

Units of measurement

Difference in means between treated and control groups with respect to different response variables:

- Willingness to pay: does the information embedded in labels/promotional material drive consumers to be willing to spend more for lower emission (in terms of type approval CO_2 emissions per km/mile) and/or fuel efficient cars or in spending less for more environmentally damaging and/or fuel inefficient ones?
- Self-reported and constructed cognitive measures of the noticeability, comprehension and recall of relevant information: consumers were asked questions on car "greenness" and fuel efficiency. Their answers were used to infer how noticeable and comprehensible information was in labels and promotional material.

Findings

Regarding labels, most findings from the lab and the stated choice experiment are inconclusive (inconsistent across treatments, indicators and engine types). However, a few more conclusive findings are worth mentioning:

- There is evidence that information on CO_2 emissions in an absolute format (i.e. where a vehicle is rated compared with vehicles from all classes) is more easily processed than information in relative format (i.e. where a vehicle is rated compared with other vehicles in the same class) or in a format combining the two.
- Treatments providing information on fuel economy seem to be more effective than treatments providing information about CO_2 emissions.

Regarding promotional materials, evidence was more robust from a statistical point of view. The most effective treatments were found to be a graphical illustration of CO_2 emissions and the salient indication of fuel costs per 5 years.

Source

Codagnone, C., F. Bogliacino and G. Veltri (2013), *Testing CO_2/Car labelling options and consumer information*, report for the European Commission, Brussels, https://ec.europa.eu/clima/sites/clima/files/transport/vehicles/labelling/docs/report_car_labelling_en.pdf.

Annex 4.A2

Framing of fuel efficiency information – Israel

Context	
Who?	Israeli Ministry of Environmental Protection
Where?	Israel
When?	June 2015
Why?	Evaluate behavioural interventions that can potentially steer car choice towards more fuel efficient alternatives.
Behavioural intervention	
Environmental policy objective	Promote private investment in more efficient technologies.
Behavioural issue	Lack of understanding of indicators of vehicle fuel efficiency. Attitude-behaviour gaps: even when consumers are aware of the meaning of fuel efficiency indicators, this may not necessarily translate into the purchase of more fuel efficient cars. Low investment in fuel efficient vehicles is also due to myopia in intertemporal choices.
Behavioural lever	Simplification and framing of information

Evaluation of the intervention: methodology

Relevant population: Israeli potential car buyers.

Sample size and sampling method(s): 350 participants (52% women), all adults (ages 25 and above, average age was 48, with a 12.5 standard deviation), were recruited from a panel of respondents.[3] Participants were potential buyers of a new family car (i.e. those who reported either purchasing a family car within the past two years, or planning to purchase one soon). Forty per cent of participants had academic education, and 53% high school education. Participants received a small pay in exchange for their participation (regardless of their answers).

Method: Stated choice experiment with within-subjects design.

Participants received a link to an internet website, where they answered a questionnaire. Part of the questionnaire was dedicated to hypothetical scenarios, where respondents were instructed to imagine that they were about to buy a new car and had to choose between the different vehicles presented to them. For each scenario of the choice experiment, two cars were shown to the participant. Altogether, participants were shown 7 pairs of cars throughout the experiment. Within each pair, the two cars differed in terms of price, fuel consumption and pollution levels (all data were based on actual details of popular car models in Israel). Participants were asked to assume that the cars were similar on all other attributes (e.g. reliability, comfort, safety, etc.).

For every pair of cars, information was presented in a different way, forming the 7 different conditions of the experiment:

- *Control 1:* fuel consumption per 100 km and pollution levels (as shown in fuel efficiency labels for cars according to current regulation).[4]
- *Control 2:* price only (in order to make sure participants understood the task).

The next 5 conditions showed the information given on conditions 1 and 2, plus additional information as follows:

- *Condition 3:* Green tax benefit. In this case, participants were shown the amount of tax benefit associated with the purchase of a given car according to its fuel efficiency level.
- *Condition 4:* Estimated fuel costs over 5 years.
- *Condition 5:* Relative loss due to additional fuel costs, as compared with the *most fuel efficient car* in the same car category/class. This leverages loss aversion.
- *Condition 6:* Difference in fuel consumption (relative loss/gain), compared to the *average* car in the same car category/class.
- *Condition 7:* Joint application of conditions 3 and 6, i.e. information on green tax benefits and difference in fuel consumption compared to average vehicle in the same class.

All participants went through all conditions at a changing and random order, including the control condition. For every pair, participants were asked to mark their preferences between the two cars on a 1 to 7 scale (1: I would certainly choose car A; 7: I would certainly choose car B).

Within each pair, one car would have a higher price, but taking into account the fuel consumption over 5 years would make it an overall better investment. For example:

	Car A	Car B
Car cost (in New Israeli Shekel)	132 000 NIS	128 300 NIS
Fuel cost for 5 years (in New Israeli Shekel)	31 610 NIS	39 520 NIS

Units of measurement: Percentage of participants choosing the most fuel efficient car under each condition.

Findings

Figure 4.A2.1 shows the percentage of participants choosing the more fuel efficient car in each condition.

Linear regression provided evidence for a statistically significant positive effect only for condition 5, which involved exposing participants to a label comparing the long-term fuel costs of each car to those required by the best-in-class car in the same category.

Surprisingly, a statistically significant negative effect was found to be associated with condition 3. Showing the tax benefit associated with the purchase of a highly fuel efficient car led to a mere 64% of consumers opting for such models. This result may seem counterintuitive, as tax benefits should incentivise the purchase of fuel efficient cars.

However, this effect may have been caused by a misunderstanding of the concept of "tax benefit" on the part of the consumers. All other conditions had no significant effect ($p<0.05$).

Intervention costs were estimated to be close to zero.

Figure 4.A2.1. **Percentage of participants choosing the most fuel efficient car under each condition**

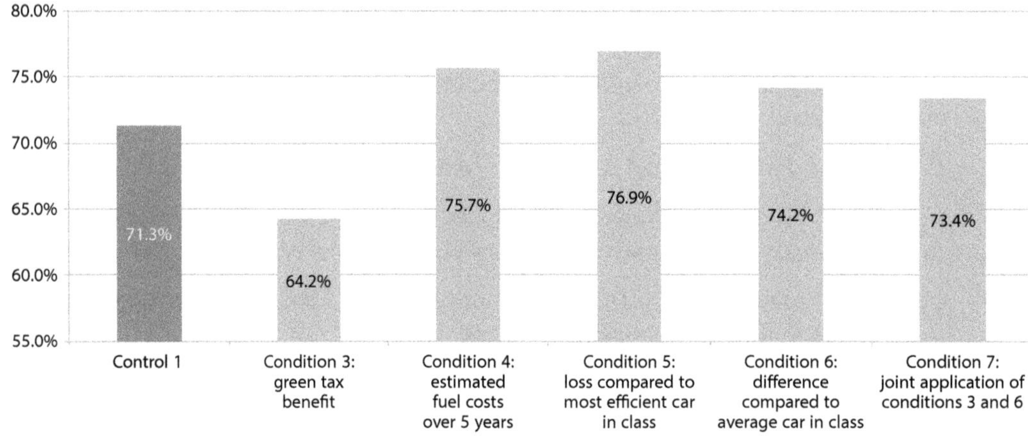

Source: documentation provided by the Israeli Ministry of Environmental Protection.

Source

Information retrieved from e-mail exchanges with the Israeli Ministry of Environmental Protection.

Notes

1. The final pollutants score, expressed on a scale from 1 to 15, is based on a formula detailed in Council Directive 80/1268/EEC of 16 December 1980 on the approximation of the laws of the Member States relating to the fuel consumption of motor vehicles. The score is computed considering mainly carbon monoxide, carbon dioxide, hydrocarbon, nitrogen oxide and particles.

2. See an overview of new label designs at https://www.epa.gov/fueleconomy/fuel-economy-and-environment-label-examples.

3. A panel of respondents is an online data base of potential participants to surveys and experiments. Candidates register voluntarily, submit their personal socio-economic details, and are often approached and offered to participate in surveys, experiments and other types of research, whether academic, commercial or governmental. Participants normally receive a small pay for the time they dedicate to participate in the study.

4. The final pollutants score, expressed on a scale from 1 to 15, is based on a formula detailed in Council Directive 80/1268/EEC of 16 December 1980 on the approximation of the laws of the Member States relating to the fuel consumption of motor vehicles. The score is computed considering mainly carbon monoxide, carbon dioxide, hydrocarbon, nitrogen oxide and particles.

References

Codagnone, C., F. Bogliacino and G. Veltri (2013), *Testing CO2/Car labelling options and consumer information*, report for the European Commission, Brussels.

Kahn, M. E. (2007), "Do greens drive Hummers or hybrids? Environmental ideology as a determinant of consumer choice", *Journal of Environmental Economics and Management*, 54(2), pp. 129–145, http://dx.doi.org/10.1016/j.jeem.2007.05.001.

Larrick, R. P. and J. B. Soll (2008), "The MPG illusion", *Science*, 320(5883), pp. 1593–1594, http://dx.doi.org/10.1126/science.1154983.

Chapter 5

Using behavioural insights to encourage water conservation

This chapter presents the behavioural interventions that have been rolled-out in order to encourage water conservation, highlighting the behavioural biases they tackle. Behavioural interventions in this area have built upon a range of behavioural levers, from reward and punishment schemes, to feedback mechanisms to salient reminders.

The behavioural biases involved in water consumption are similar to the ones outlined in the discussion of energy consumption developed in Chapter 3: *status-quo bias*, *attitude-behaviour gap due to cognitive dissonances*, and *framing effects* (see Reader's Guide for definitions of all technical terms). Besides these behavioural elements, some features of the water market make it more complex for consumers to match specific water consumption choices to their cost. Salience of water meters is a specific issue in this context: households without an individual meter cannot track their consumption. Furthermore, feedback via bills tends to be infrequent and not as detailed.

Based on the research backing this report, it appears that few behavioural interventions have been implemented in this field, possibly because water conservation is not ranked as high as energy efficiency in the policy agenda across countries. For this reason, these interventions have not had large-scale impacts on the policy making sphere. Furthermore, it is interesting to note that two of the three behavioural interventions reviewed in this policy area are from developing countries: this may be due to relatively lower water security levels in these countries.

Social norms and comparisons are the behavioural lever that has been applied in Costa Rica and in Colombia. On the one hand, comparisons with similar households were introduced in water bills in Costa Rica. On the other hand, public rewards and penalties for specific water consumption behaviours have been deployed in Colombia. The intervention implemented in Switzerland instead leverages the use of *feedback mechanisms*.

Changes to the physical environment and reward & punishment schemes to encourage water conservation

In 1997, the city of Bogotá suffered from a water shortage due to an infrastructural failure of the tunnel connecting the capital to its main freshwater source for several months. Trying to promote water savings in an emergency situation, the city authorities took several actions. The first initiative was a communication campaign to convey the magnitude of the emergency, which could leave 70% of the city without water. Contrary to policy makers' expectations, an increase in water use was observed in the aftermath of this campaign. While multiple factors may have contributed to this, a possible explanation of the communication campaign's failure to deliver an immediate reduction in water consumption is that Bogotá's inhabitants were not convinced that they could make a difference and did not know where to start saving water.

Changing communication strategy, city authorities implemented three different types of interventions simultaneously:

- *Changes to the physical environment*: distribution of stickers to place next to water faucets in order to make the need to conserve water salient at the point of use.
- *Reward and punishment schemes*: public rewards for households attaining particularly high water savings, publicising their strategies, and fines for water squanderers.
- *Information provision*: campaign to spread information on the most effective ways to save water. This was a standard information campaign, in that it was not behaviourally informed.
- These interventions helped create a social norm of water conservation, which led to actual savings beyond the most optimistic predictions: 8 weeks after the beginning of the campaign, total water savings peaked at 13.8%. It is important to note that the assessment of these policy interventions, carried out without a solid counterfactual,

does not allow detecting a causal link between them and the decrease in water consumption, which may have also been affected by other confounding factors. It is also impossible to disentangle the effect of each of the three interventions. Given these caveats in terms of evaluation, this policy initiative is based on interesting examples of behaviourally informed interventions.

- While these interventions were launched as a reaction to an emergency situation, they turned out to impact water consumption – a typically routine behaviour – in the longer run. In fact, impacts of the information campaign persisted well beyond the end of the water scarcity emergency: per capita water consumption remained below pre-crisis levels for over a decade (World Bank, 2015).

Testing social comparisons and goal setting for water savings

In July 2014, the city of Belén in Costa Rica ran a field experiment jointly with think tank *ideas42* and the World Bank to assess the impact of social comparisons and feedback provision on water consumption. Water conservation is a priority for the local municipality, given the risk of water shortage the city may incur in the near future (Datta et al., 2015 – see also Annex 5.A1).

More specifically, the randomised controlled trial tested three alternative behavioural levers:

a. *Neighbourhood-level social comparison:* stickers on the water bill providing a comparison of one's own water consumption to that of the average household in the same neighbourhood.

b. *City-level social comparison:* stickers on the water bill providing a comparison of one's own energy consumption to that of the average household in Belén.

c. *Goal-setting and plan-making:* worksheet making relative consumption salient and prompting consumers to write down a personal goal to reduce water consumption. The worksheet also provided tips to reach these goals.

The trial showed that two of three levers had statistically significant impacts on water consumption, leading to its reduction in the months following the intervention. Neighbourhood comparison reduced water consumption by 3.7-5.6% relative to the control group. On the other hand, the comparison with the average Belén household turned out to be ineffective: the authors explain this by the fact that more localised and specific norms (e.g. neighbourhood-level social comparison) are more effective in prompting behavioural change (Datta et al., 2015).

Goal-setting and plan-making reduced consumption by 3.4-5.5% relative to the control group. It is important to note that, while yielding broadly similar results, these two behavioural levers vary in their impact across different subpopulations. More precisely, plan-making appears to be most effective for low-consumption households, who may already be motivated for water conservation efforts and just need support in identifying concrete actions. Conversely, neighbourhood comparison is most effective for high-consumption households, who may not have a clear sense of how their water consumption patterns compare to their peers ex ante (Datta et al., 2015).

Feedback mechanisms for water conservation

In 2012, the Swiss Federal Office of Energy commissioned a field experiment assessing the impact of real-time feedback on hot water consumption from showers on individual behaviour (see also Annex 5.A2). Real-time feedback was provided to consumers via an in-shower smart meter indicating the water and energy consumption of the ongoing shower and/or the previous one. Control group participants were instead exposed solely to information on water temperature, and did not receive real-time feedback on water nor on energy consumption.

Real-time feedback led to a statistically significant reduction in average water and energy consumption by about 23% compared to the control group. Following this finding, the authors tried to pin down what behavioural changes were prompted by feedback provision. They found that the main behavioural adjustment at the root of reduced hot water consumption was a decrease in shower duration by over 20%. Conversely, adjustments of water temperature and flow rate or repeated stops of the water flow were not found to play such a significant role, albeit contributing to conservation. Individuals with higher (i.e. above-median) baseline consumption to begin with, reacted to the intervention with stronger behavioural change, leading to a larger decrease in hot water consumption in absolute terms (Tiefenbeck et al., 2014).

Conclusion on water conservation

Two of the interventions reviewed in this chapter have been motivated by emergency situations, to prompt fast behavioural adaptations to sudden water crises (Bogotá, Colombia), and by preventive approaches, aimed at introducing more conservative water consumption behaviours to avoid water scarcity in the longer run (Belén, Costa Rica). The third instead connects water and energy conservation issues (Switzerland).

The field experiment methodology has been popular in this context: the indicators and meters to monitor water consumption are already in place, as in the energy field.

The interventions implemented in the water sector point to the effectiveness of social norms and comparisons, salient reminders (modest changes to the physical environment) and goal setting paired with clear action tips in prompting water conservation. In the case of Bogotá, water saving behaviour prompted by behavioural interventions rolled out in an emergency context has proven to be remarkably persistent, making a dent in routine behaviours. These findings somehow mirror results from interventions implemented in the energy sector, even though they have not prompted large-scale policy changes (World Bank, 2015).

An important take-home from the Belén case study but with relevance beyond the water policy domain is that different behavioural interventions may have different impacts on heterogeneous social groups. For this reason, it is worth zooming in on subgroups, in order to understand to what extent the effectiveness of behavioural interventions varies and to take this variation into account when implementing a policy scheme. It is also interesting to note that the choice of benchmark group may be critical for the effectiveness of the intervention (Datta et al., 2015).

The intervention from Switzerland uses feedback mechanisms to curb hot water consumption in the shower. These mechanisms were shown to successfully drive both water conservation and energy efficiency, achieving a twofold objective. In this case too, subgroup analysis has provided useful insights into the behavioural changes driven by the intervention (e.g. differences between high/low water consumption groups, young/old individuals) (Tiefenbeck et al., 2014).

Annex 5.A1

Testing social norms and feedback provision for water savings – Costa Rica

Context	
Who?	Municipality of Belén. Study realised by think tank *ideas42* and the World Bank.
Where?	Belén, Costa Rica
When?	July 2014
Why?	This field experiment aimed at testing different interventions to foster water savings: comparisons based on social norms and goal setting and plan-making interventions.
Intervention type	
Environmental policy objective	Encourage conservation of resources
Behavioural issue	Status-quo bias and cognitive dissonances can prevent consumers from increasing conservation efforts. Furthermore, infrequent feedback provision via bills and scarce visibility of meters are market features why make it difficult for consumers to connect their consumption patterns with their actual price, hindering conservation efforts.
Behavioural lever	Use of social comparisons; Goal setting and commitment devices.

Evaluation of the intervention: methodology

Relevant population: Residential water consumers in Belén, Costa Rica.

Sample size and sampling method(s): All individually-metered households in Belén (5626 households).

Method: Field experiment designed as randomised controlled trial.

Participants were randomly assigned to 3 treatment groups and a control group.

The treatments were:

a. *Neighbourhood comparison*: stickers on the water bill providing comparison of a household's consumption to that of the benchmark household in the same neighbourhood.

b. *City comparison*: stickers on the water bill providing comparison of a household's consumption to that of the benchmark household in the city of Belén.

c. *Goal-setting and plan-making*: worksheet making current and past consumption salient and prompting water consumers to write down a personal goal to reduce water consumption, providing tips to reach these goals.

Units of measurement: Percentage change in the average post-intervention relative to pre-intervention water consumption. The outcome is measured as the average of the water consumption in the 2 months following the intervention.

Findings

- The neighbourhood comparison intervention reduced water consumption by 3.7 to 5.6% relative to the control group.
- The goal-setting and plan-making intervention led to water consumption reductions by 3.4 to 5.5%.
- The city comparison intervention did not lead to statistically significant results.

The effectiveness of the interventions was tested also in different subsamples: this highlighted that goal-setting and plan-making seems to be most effective for low-consumption households, whereas neighbourhood comparison seems to be most effective for high-consumption households.

Regarding intervention costs, the cost of printing out the stickers and worksheets was USD 400. The study estimates that extending one of the two effective treatments (neighbourhood comparison and plan-making) to all individually metered households in Belen would yield a benefit/cost ratio from 6.5 to 13, with the monetary benefits of household water savings largely surpassing the costs of expanding the interventions.

Source

Datta, S. et al. (2015), "A Behavioral Approach to Water Conservation. Evidence from Costa Rica." *Policy Research working paper*; no. WPS 7283, Impact Evaluation series, World Bank Group, Washington, DC, http://documents.worldbank.org/curated/en/809801468001190306/A-behavioral-approach-to-water-conservation-evidence-from-Costa-Rica.

Annex 5.A2

Real time feedback on hot water consumption in the shower – Switzerland

Context	
Who?	Swiss Federal Office of Energy, study developed by researchers at ETH Zurich and University of Lausanne in collaboration with ETH Zurich spin-off company Amphiro AG and utility company *ewz*. The real time feedback device was developed with the support of the Federal Office for the Environment (FOEN).
Where?	Switzerland
When?	Early December 2012 – early February 2013 (2 months)
Why?	Investigate the impact of real time feedback mechanisms on hot water consumption in the shower (i.e. volume of water consumed and average temperature).
Behavioural intervention	
Environmental policy objective	Encourage conservation of resources
Behavioural issue	Status-quo bias and cognitive dissonances can prevent consumers from increasing conservation efforts. Furthermore, infrequent feedback provision via bills and scarce visibility of meters are market features making it difficult for consumers to link their consumption patterns with their costs, hindering conservation efforts.
Behavioural lever	Use of feedback mechanisms

Evaluation of the intervention: methodology

Relevant population: One and two-person Swiss households.

Sample size and sampling method(s): 697 households selected among customers of utility company *ewz*, partner of the study. Participation was limited to households with maximum 2 members, because devices could store data on a limited number of showers.

Households voluntarily opted into the experiment by filling in a survey, after having received information on the project from *ewz*.

Method: field experiment designed as a randomised controlled trial.

Participating households were randomly assigned to three groups, each of which received a different version of the smart shower meter "amphiro a1", offering different feedback information through its in-shower monitor:

- Control group: meter showing only temperature.
- Treatment group 1: meter showing temperature and real-time feedback on current water and energy consumption.
- Treatment group 2: meter showing temperature, real-time feedback on current water and energy consumption and feedback on water consumption relative to the previous shower.

Surveys were carried out before and after the experiment. Among other things, the ex-ante survey involved questions on demographics, environmental attitudes, and the pricing rates to which the household was subject for water and heat (e.g. flat rate vs. rate varying with consumption). The ex-post survey instead aimed at understanding how the participants perceived their experience with the smart water meter.

Units of measurement:

- Litres of water consumed per shower.
- kWh of thermal energy consumed per shower (for the production of hot water).

Findings

The authors empirically assessed the impact of the introduction of the smart water meter on a) water consumed per shower and b) energy consumed per shower (calculated on the basis of the volume of water user per shower and its average temperature).

The baseline information is based on the first ten showers, during which all users where exposed to the same information. Starting from the 11th shower, individuals in the treatment groups were exposed to real-time information. Data collection lasted 2 months.

Water consumption: Among 1-person households, exposure to real-time information reduced water consumption per shower by 9.4 litres relative to the control group. Exposure to real-time and past information led to larger water savings, reducing water consumption by 10.4 litres. Both effects were statistically significant at the 10% level. Comparable savings were reported when it comes to 2-person households (respectively -10.4 and -10.9 litres of water).

As the average water consumption per shower in the control group was 44 litres, these savings reduced average water consumption by about 23%. The magnitude of the effect was virtually the same in 1-person and 2-person households.

Energy consumption: Both in 1-person and 2-person households, the two treatments led to statistically significant ($p<0.01$) energy savings between 0.3 and 0.4 kWh per shower.[1] This amount translates into about 5% of a household's daily energy consumption.

Behavioural patterns: reducing water use during a shower can be accomplished by shortening its duration, pausing water flow or reducing the flow rate; reducing energy use instead can also be accomplished by reducing the temperature of water during the shower. The authors tested the impacts of the different interventions on each of these behavioural choices:

- *Duration of shower*: in the control group, the average duration of a shower was 245 seconds (about 4 minutes). Treatment exposure resulted in statistically significant ($p<0.01$) reductions of shower duration by 45 to 55 seconds (about 18-22%).
- *Flow rate during a shower (litres per minute)*: the average flow rate in the control groups was around 11 litres per minute, regardless of household size. The treatments led to a statistically significant decrease in the water flow rate of about 0.3 litres per minute among 1-person households. No statistically significant results were found among 2-person households.
- *Water temperature*: average water temperature in the control group was 36 degrees. In the 1-person household group, the two treatments led to statistically significant reductions between 0.4 and 0.7 degrees Celsius. Again, no statistically significant

results were found among 2-person households. The authors thus state that "as with the flow rate, the temperature doesn't appear to be an important margin of adjustment." (Tiefenbeck et al., 2014, p. 51).

- *Pauses in water flow*: the water flow was stopped on average for 30 to 35 seconds per shower in the control group, depending on the type of households. Showing real-time information on water consumption led to statistically significant longer pauses by 9 seconds among 2-person households only.

Overall, the two interventions led to a statistically significant decrease (-23%) in water and energy consumption per shower. Following the analysis of behavioural drivers of this reduction, the authors state that "change in behavior is primarily driven by a change in the duration of the shower by over 20 percent. Other margins of adjustment, such as flow rate, water temperature, or stops of water flow during a shower, all point in the direction of more conservation, but fail to show a clear and important contribution to the overall outcome that we observed." (Tiefenbeck et al., 2014, p. 51).

Impact differences across subgroups: the intervention seems to be more effective (i.e. to drive a stronger behavioural response) among individuals with high baseline consumption and among individuals predisposed to goal-setting and monitoring. For example, 20-29 year-olds consumed 72% more resources per shower (baseline) than participants over 65, but responded to the intervention with larger consumption cuts.

Environmental attitudes of participants were not shown to significantly affect the overall net impact of the intervention.

While it was apparent that the intervention increased awareness about water consumption patterns, it did not seem that consumers reacted to the "negative psychological pressure" that might have been induced by the new meters. For example, households receiving information the previous shower did not seem to have a stronger reaction to meter prompts: peer pressure did not seem to be an important driver of behavioural change.

Note

1. This figure assumes 100% boiler efficiency and zero losses in generation, distribution and storage: it represents a lower bound of actual energy savings. Actual boiler efficiency depends on boiler size and age, as well as fuel type.

Source

Tiefenbeck, V. et al. (2014), *On the effectiveness of real-time feedback: The influence of demographics, attitudes, and personality traits*, report for the Swiss Federal Office of Energy, Bern.

References

Datta, S. et al. (2015), "A Behavioral Approach to Water Conservation. Evidence from Costa Rica." *Policy Research working paper*; no. WPS 7283, Impact Evaluation series, World Bank Group, Washington, DC, http://documents.worldbank.org/curated/en/809801468001190306/A-behavioral-approach-to-water-conservation-evidence-from-Costa-Rica.

Tiefenbeck, V. et al. (2014), *On the effectiveness of real-time feedback: The influence of demographics, attitudes, and personality traits*, report for the Swiss Federal Office of Energy, Bern.

World Bank (2015), *World Development Report 2015: Mind, Society and Behavior*, Washington, DC, doi: 10.1596/978-1-4648-0342-0.

Chapter 6

Using behavioural insights to incentivise environmentally sustainable food consumption

This chapter presents behavioural interventions rolled-out to encourage more sustainable food consumption. The behavioural biases at play are highlighted, together with the behavioural levers used by policy makers to tackle them. Interventions in this area have focused on two main issues: informing consumers about the environmental footprint of their food choices, and limiting food waste through persuasive messages.

Food purchase and consumption choices are affected by several information issues: grocery products typically carry multiple indicators of differing complexity, ranging from the expiration date to the nutritional value or the environmental footprint of a product. *Cognitive limitations* (see Reader's Guide for definitions of all technical terms) make it difficult to pay attention to all these criteria: information overload may lead consumers to focus on a couple of criteria, which may be simpler and of more immediate understanding, e.g. price, colour or appearance. Furthermore, even a motivated and environmentally conscious consumer may have trouble in fully understanding all these indicators, or in translating vague invitations to engage in sustainable consumption into concrete product choices. This may lead to an *attitude behaviour gap*. Finally, *social norms* have a fundamental impact on food choice and consumption, as these behaviours are deeply entrenched in cultural elements. Eating individually or within a group implies different food choices.

Applications of behavioural insights in this area have revolved around testing the impact of framing on consumers' understanding of complex indicators such as those described above, as well as on their ultimate purchase and consumption choices. The following three applications were part of a broader behavioural study ordered by the Consumers, Health, Agriculture and Food Executive Agency (CHAFEA) on behalf of the European Commission to test consumer choices in relation to food sustainability and drivers of food waste (ECORYS, Tilburg University and GfK, 2015).

Framing sustainability information to encourage environmentally conscious grocery shopping

This intervention took place in July 2015 at the "Supermarket of the Future", a grocery store within the Milan Universal Exposition (see also Annex 6.A1). This shop contained interactive screens through which consumers could access additional information on a variety of product features: price, product history, origin of raw materials used, nutritional values, allergy information, environmental information, and logos indicating the product's carbon footprint, whether it is organic and its sustainability (environmental impact of the production process and social responsibility of the producer). Given this setting was an artificial reconstruction of a supermarket (albeit with innovative tweaks) and as visitors were motivated to enter it by the discovery interest rather than by consumption needs, this is a peculiar field experiment of food choice. Rather, the objective of this experiment was two-fold:

- To assess to what extent and in what way consumers exploited the information conveyed through interactive screens in their purchase decisions. More specifically, the experiment aimed at testing whether exposing consumers to sustainability-related information in an innovative, interactive way (e.g. via interactive screens) steered them towards more sustainable food choices.
- To assess whether sustainable actions in non-food domains affect consumption choices in the food domain. This was tested by exposing consumers to an activity that was expected to activate their sustainability behaviour prior to their visit to the supermarket (a "sustainability pre-task").

The field experiment was designed as a between-subject intervention, meaning that participants were randomly assigned to one of three groups (two treatment groups and one control group, of about 100 participants each). The treatment for the first group consisted solely of a visit to the supermarket, which was characterised by multiple changes to the physical environment (e.g. interactive screens featuring sustainability information on food products) in comparison to standard grocery stores. Treatment for the second group paired a visit to the supermarket with a sustainability task. For various non-food product categories, this task consisted e.g. in choosing the most sustainable product. This prompted consumers to actively think about the environmental impact of various goods. Finally, participants to the control group were only asked to answer a questionnaire and exposed to charity donation choice, as the other two groups after the supermarket visit. The post-visit questionnaire gathered information on attention paid to sustainability information throughout the supermarket (self-reported measure), on the importance that respondents attributed to sustainability information in food choice and on their sustainable behaviour. It also questioned participants about whether and how they would make more sustainable food choices in the future.

The experiment led to four main sets of results:

- When questioned about the product information elements they paid more attention to while at the supermarket, visitors pointed to price, nutritional value and origin of raw materials rather than sustainability information. This is in line with elements pointed to by consumers unexposed to the visit, signalling that the setup of the Supermarket itself did not lead consumers to more attentively consider sustainability features of products.
- However, store visitors tended to state stronger intentions to take the environmental footprint into consideration in future shopping relatively to non-visitors.
- The experiment did not deliver evidence in favour of spill-overs from the non-food to the food domain. In fact, consumers exposed to sustainability pre-tasks did not significantly differ from the control group in the attention paid to sustainability or in the importance associated with it in the purchase context.
- Finally, when faced with the choice of three charities to which they could donate at the end of the questionnaire, supermarket visitors tended to donate more than non-visitors to charities active in the sustainability sector.

Framing durability and authenticity information to reduce food waste

Food waste can be countered both at the product choice and at the product consumption stage. This can be done by framing information on the correct way to store produce to preserve its quality and taste, as well as by framing information on product durability and characteristics if correctly preserved.

This set of lab experiments aimed at uncovering the factors that can increase consumer acceptance of imperfect foods (not perfect-looking but of high standards in terms of taste and quality) at the product choice stage (see also Annex 6.A2). Two types of messages were tested to assess their impact on consumer behaviour and their effectiveness relatively to price discounts in inducing consumers to purchase imperfect produce:

- An anti-food-waste message, encouraging consumers to act against food waste by adhering to the purchase of imperfect produce.
- An authenticity message, underlining that imperfect produce is natural and therefore has the same qualities as perfect-looking produce.

The experiment was designed as a between-subjects intervention, whereby 500 participants were divided into six groups by random assignment. The six groups were exposed to one of two messages and one of three specific price scenarios at a time (2 by 3 design), in which imperfect produce was sold either at the same price as perfect produce, with a moderate price reduction (15% cheaper) or with a sharper price reduction (30% cheaper).

The experiment showed that exposing consumers to awareness-raising messages can increase their intention to buy imperfect produce. The effectiveness of the anti-food-waste message relatively to the authenticity message depended on the price change to which they were associated:

- *Preference for imperfect produce:*
  - *Same price*: with no price reductions, both messages had roughly the same effectiveness, leading about 41% of consumers to opt for imperfect produce, a substantially higher opt-in rate than in the control group exposed solely to the price tag (26%).
  - *Moderate price reduction*: the anti-food waste message led to 51% of consumers opting for imperfect produce, 11 percentage points above the share of consumers opting in following the authenticity message and 20 percentage points above the share of consumers opting in without any message exposure.
  - *Sharp price reduction*: both messages deliver roughly the same impact (50-51% of consumers opting for imperfect produce as opposed to 39% in the control group).
- *Persuasive messages vs price discounts*: persuasive messages can play an important role in alternative or in conjunction with price discounts. The above findings show that an anti-food waste message can deliver the same impact at a moderate and at a sharp price reduction: about 50% of consumers opting for imperfect produce over perfect produce.
- *Perceived quality:* Both types of messages increased the perceived quality of imperfect produce. Interestingly, an authenticity message led to a higher perceived quality of imperfect produce when no discount was offered.

These results can inform actions aimed at reducing food waste at the store level. To complement these insights, a different lab experiment studied how the decision to use or dispose of non-perishable long shelf-life food items is affected by the presence or absence of dates indicating product durability (e.g. production or best-before date) on food labels (see also Annex 6.A3).

The experiment was designed as a between-subjects intervention, whereby 500 participants were divided into six groups by random assignment. Groups differed in whether they would be exposed to couples of non-perishable consumption goods (juice, sauce, pasta, coffee) with a best-before date, a production date or no date at all, and in whether the perceived shelf life of the product was long or short. Consumers would need to indicate their willingness to consume or throw away each of the two products to which they were exposed, as well as their perceived product quality and safety.

The lab experiment led to the following results:

- *Understanding of best-before dates:* Only 47% of experiment participants correctly understood the meaning of best-before date (optimal quality guarantee).
- *Disposal probability:* Intuitively, showing a BBD was effective in preventing waste before it was reached, while it led to higher likelihood of disposal after its occurrence. This means that ultimately, the likelihood of disposing of products when they were marked with a best-before date depended on how long consumers typically kept

long-lived products (e.g. pasta, coffee) in their cupboard before consuming them, while this was less of an issue for short-lived products (e.g. orange juice, pasta sauce). For this reason, it was complex to assess whether a best-before date was preferable to no date at all. On the other hand, providing a production date was shown to be less effective (for long-lived products) or equally effective (for short-lived products) in reducing the probability of product disposal compared to no date mark.

- *Perceived product safety and quality:* Showing a best-before date has a positive impact on the perception of safety and quality (and is preferred to showing a production date or no date) until the best-before date is reached; after this date, showing no date leads to higher perceived quality and safety.

Conclusion on food consumption

In the food consumption domain, the behavioural insights applications reviewed in this report have been based on simplifying and framing information related to food products (e.g. environmental impact and quality guarantee indicators). They have mainly been implemented via lab and field experiments (ECORYS, Tilburg University and GfK, 2015).

These experiments indicate that environmental sustainability is not by default one of the main driving criteria for food purchases. Increasing its salience and relevance may help, while also ensuring that sustainability indicators are well understood by consumers. It has also been shown that encouraging environmentally sustainable food choices does not necessarily generate spill-overs, meaning it does not drive greener consumption patterns in the non-food compartment.

A way to reduce food waste at the product choice stage is to incentivise the purchase of imperfect produce, preventing it from going to waste. In this context, a persuasive message inviting consumers to purchase imperfect-looking food products in order to prevent food waste has been shown to be effective even without substantial cutting these products' prices.

If the sustainability of food products is not automatically considered at purchase, one alternative way to reduce the environmental impact of food consumption is to ensure that no food goes wasted after it has been bought. For this reason it is important to ensure that consumers have a correct understanding of food labels (e.g. best-before dates), which impacts their perception of quality and durability of produce.

One of the lab experiments analysed above shows that framing the optimal quality guarantee by best-before date or production date makes a difference in terms of disposal probability and perceived safety and quality of groceries. This is due to the incomplete understanding that consumers have of these indicators. This highlights the need to simplify them in order to ensure that consumers avoid throwing away groceries while they are still perfectly safe for consumption. These insights have already started to impact the policy process: the European Commission, for instance, is considering simplifying date markings on food produce.[1]

Annex 6.A1

Consumer use of sustainability information – European Commission

Context	
Who?	Study developed by ECORYS, Tilburg University and GfK, ordered by the Consumers, Health, Agriculture and Food Executive Agency (CHAFEA) on behalf of the European Commission.
Where?	Universal Exposition, Milan, Italy
When?	2015 (data collection between June 30 and July 6)
Why?	This field experiment is part of a broader behavioural study that tested consumer choices in relation to food sustainability. The objective of the experiment was to investigate the impact of exposing consumers to sustainability-related information on their food choices.
Behavioural intervention	
Environmental policy objective	Incentivise environmentally sustainable consumption patterns
Behavioural issue	Consumer use of sustainability information in the context of food choice
Behavioural lever	Simplification and framing of information

Evaluation of the intervention: methodology

Relevant population: Visitors of the Milan 2015 Universal Exposition.

Sample size and sampling method: 303 participants, randomly picked among visitors of the Exposition.

Method: field experiment based on a between-subject design.

The experiment took place in the "Supermarket of the Future" at the Milan Universal Exposition. This supermarket contained interactive screens on which consumers could access, alongside standard features (e.g. price, nutritional values, allergy information), additional features such as the origin of raw materials used, environmental information and the carbon footprint, organic and sustainability logos.

With random assignment, the participants were divided into three groups (about 100 participants per group) and exposed to a combination of the following treatments:

- Sustainability behaviour activation activity (group 1),
- Visit to the Supermarket of the Future (group 1 and 2),
- Post-visit questionnaire at the exit of the supermarket (group 1 and 2) or in another area of Expo (group 3, non-visitors) and possibility of donating to charities.

Group 3 was the control group, untreated with the visit to the Supermarket of the future

The exposure of the various groups of participants to the treatments is summarised in Table 6.A1.1.

Table 6.A1.1. **Treatment allocation**

Group	Pre-visit contact	Visit	Post-visit contact
1	Sustainable behaviour activation	Supermarket of the future	Questionnaire + Donation behaviour
2		Supermarket of the future	Questionnaire + Donation behaviour
3			Questionnaire + Donation behaviour

Source: adapted from ECORYS, Tilburg University and GfK (2015). © European Union, 2015. Reproduction is authorised provided the source is acknowledged.

Units of measurement: The impact of the intervention on consumers' attention and on the stated importance of product information for their future choices was measured by observing the following:

- Stated level of attention and importance for price, nutritional values, origin raw materials, carbon footprint, sustainability logos, organic logos.
- Statement on whether this information is used to base current and future purchase decisions on.
- Stated likelihood to take into account the above-mentioned elements for future purchases.
- Stated intentions to take environmental concerns into account.

Furthermore, the impact assessment also studied charity donation behaviour: at the end of the questionnaire, consumers could donate to a charity of their choice among: i) a charity related to sustainability in the food domain (Fairfood); ii) a charity pursuing sustainability in general (One Acre); and iii) a charity outside of the sustainability domain (Age international).

Findings

The authors of the study find that "Store visitors paid more attention to the price, nutritional values and origin of raw materials than to the sustainability information components [...]. In the same vein, price, nutritional values and origin of raw materials are considered more important to consumers than sustainability" (ECORYS, Tilburg University and GfK, 2015). Figures 6.A1.1 and 6.A1.2 show the levels of attention and the importance that consumers associate with various features represented in the interactive screens:

The authors also report that "[c]onsumers intend to put relatively more weight to sustainability information compared to the other informational attributes (price, nutritional value, original raw materials) in the future [...]. In addition, store visitors have stronger intentions to take environmental concerns into account in future shopping than non-visitors." (ECORYS, Tilburg University and GfK, 2015). This is represented in Figure 6.A1.2.

Finally, when it came to charity donations, it was found that "supermarket visitors (group 1 and 2) donate more to sustainable charities than non-visitors (group 3). That is, non-visitors spread their donation more equally over all three charities" (ECORYS, Tilburg University and GfK, 2015). This insight is represented in Figure 6.A1.3.

Figure 6.A1.1. **Consumer attention and importance for information components**

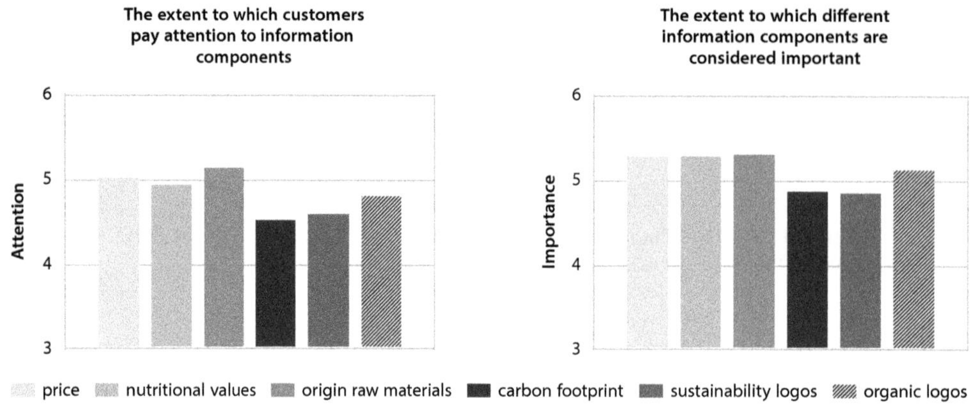

Source: ECORYS, Tilburg University and GfK (2015). © European Union, 2015. Reproduction is authorised provided the source is acknowledged.

Figure 6.A1.2. **Consumer use of information in purchase decisions**

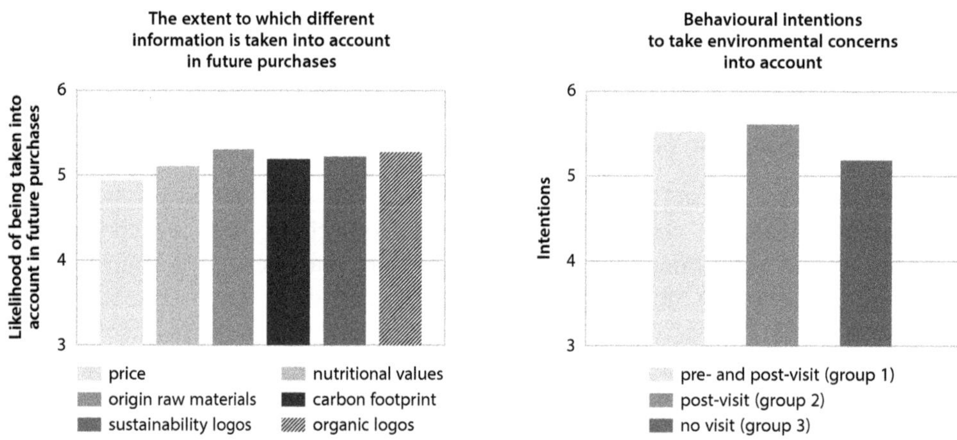

Source: ECORYS, Tilburg University and GfK (2015). © European Union, 2015. Reproduction is authorised provided the source is acknowledged.

Figure 6.A1.3. **Amount donated per charity**

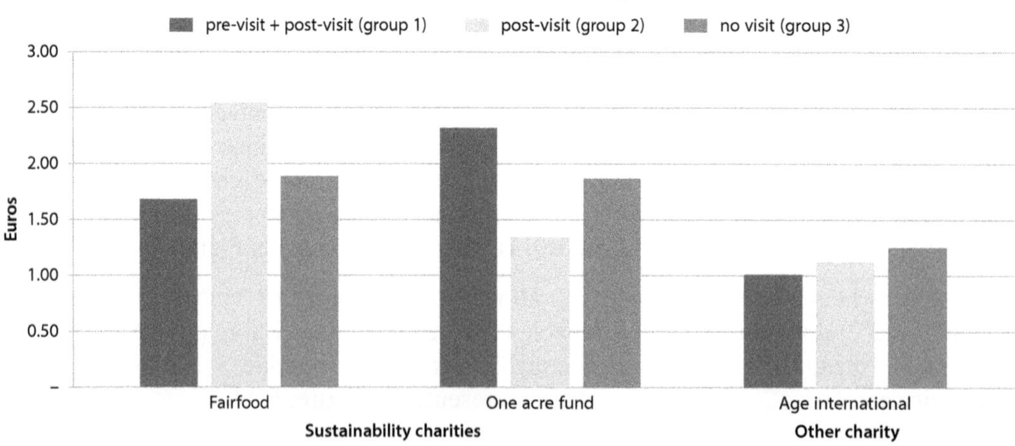

Source: ECORYS, Tilburg University and GfK (2015). © European Union, 2015. Reproduction is authorised provided the source is acknowledged.

Source

ECORYS, Tilburg University and GfK (2015), *Milan BExpo 2015 : A behavioural study on food choices and eating habits*, report for the European Commission, Brussels, http://dx.doi.org/10.2838/537411.

Annex 6.A2

Food waste and imperfect produce – European Commission

Context	
Who?	Study developed by ECORYS, Tilburg University and GfK, ordered by the Consumers, Health, Agriculture and Food Executive Agency (CHAFEA) on behalf of the European Commission.
Where?	Universal Exposition, Milan, Italy.
When?	2015 (data collection between June 30 and July 6).
Why?	This lab experiment is part of a broader behavioural study tested consumer choices in relation to food sustainability. More precisely, this intervention aimed at uncovering the factors that can increase consumer acceptance of imperfect food (not perfect looking but with optimal taste and quality).
Behavioural intervention	
Environmental policy objective	Incentivise environmentally sustainable consumption patterns.
Behavioural issue	The preference for perfect-looking produce may be due to a non-evidence-based belief that imperfect-looking produce is associated with lower taste and quality.
Behavioural lever	Simplification and framing of information.

Evaluation of the intervention: methodology

Relevant population: Visitors of the Milan 2015 Universal Exposition.

Sample size and sampling method(s): 500 participants (mostly Italian), randomly picked among visitors of the Exposition. Note that the sample is very limited both in size and in nationalities represented.

Method: Lab experiment with a 2 by 3 between-subjects design.

Participants were shown one of two types of message in the context of the purchase of apples and carrots:

- Anti-food-waste messages, e.g. "Embrace imperfection: join the fight against food waste!"
- Authenticity messages, stressing that the food is "naturally imperfect".

Both of these messages were combined with three price scenarios: a) no price reduction for imperfect food, b) moderate price reduction (15%) for imperfect food, or c) sharp price reduction (30%) for imperfect food.

Treatment selection was randomly assigned and the control group was not exposed to any awareness-raising message (i.e. participants in this group were only exposed to one of the three price scenarios).

Units of measurement: Percentage of consumers willing to buy imperfect food following exposure to different messages/price reductions.

Findings

Awareness-raising messages have been shown to increase participants' intention to buy imperfect food (in this case, apples and carrots). Likewise, and very intuitively, price reductions have the same effect. The experiment shows that a combination of price reductions and promotional messages leads to an even higher intention to buy imperfect food. The most effective promotional message depends on the price level to which consumers are simultaneously exposed. This is shown in Figure 6.A2.1 and, because no differences were found between carrots and apples, the results are presented jointly:

Figure 6.A2.1. **Percentage of consumers buying imperfect and perfect food**

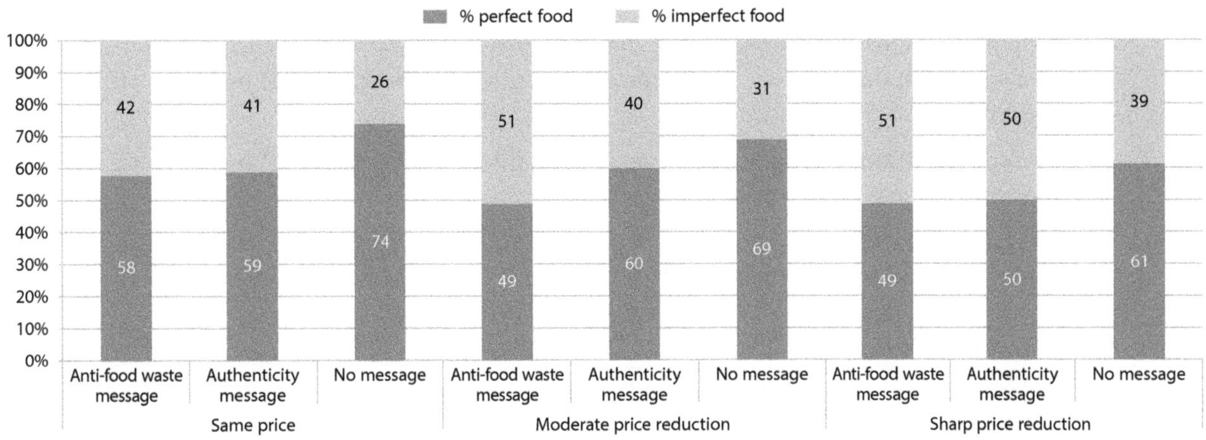

Source: ECORYS, Tilburg University and GfK (2015). © European Union, 2015. Reproduction is authorised provided the source is acknowledged.

Price reductions

The study found that, intuitively, the share of consumers willing to buy imperfect food increased with the magnitude of the price reduction. As shown in Figure 6.A2.1, the following patterns could be observed when participants were not exposed to any persuasive message:

- When perfect and imperfect food was sold at the *same price*, 74% of consumers would buy perfect food, while 26% would buy imperfect food.
- When imperfect food was sold at a *moderate price reduction*, the share of consumers willing to buy it slightly increased to 31%.
- Finally, when imperfect food was sold at a *sharp price reduction*, this share reached 39%.

Persuasive messages

The impact of exposing consumers to persuasive messages is visible in the same-price scenario: when exposed to no such message, 74% of consumers would buy perfect food while 26% would buy imperfect food. Under the same price scenario, introducing an authenticity message or anti-food waste message respectively brought the share of consumers willing to buy imperfect food to 41% and 42%. The impact of both persuasive messages was ultimately found to be very similar when perfect and imperfect food products were sold at the same price.

Combining price reductions with persuasive messages

Exposing consumers to both price changes and persuasive messages allowed to study whether the presence of the latter may reduce the necessity of price reductions to provide incentives for imperfect food consumption. In fact, the authors of the study state that "[a] lower price of food is often used as a justification by consumers to throw food away." (ECORYS, Tilburg University and GfK, 2015, p. 28)

Combining price reductions with anti-food or authenticity messages increased willingness to pay for imperfect food: as shown in Figure 6.A2.1,

- Without any message, 31% of participants would buy the imperfect food with a moderate price reduction, and 39% of participants would buy imperfect food with a sharp price reduction;
- With an authenticity message, the share of consumers willing to purchase imperfect food at a moderate price reduction would increase to 40%; this share would hit 50% with a sharp price reduction;
- With an anti-food waste message, this share would jump to 51% both with a moderate and a sharp price reduction.

Ultimately, the authors of the study recommended pairing a moderate price reduction with a message frame, where the anti-food waste message seemed to be most effective.

Quality perception

"[B]oth extrinsic (anti-food waste) and intrinsic (authenticity) message framing leads to increased quality perceptions for imperfect foods, but [...] for intrinsic message framing to yield higher quality perceptions, a price reduction is not necessary (and may in fact diminish the effect)" (ECORYS, Tilburg University and GfK, 2015, p. 30). This is pictured in Figure 6.A2.2, which shows the product quality perception for imperfect apples.

Figure 6.A2.2. **Product quality perception for imperfect apples**

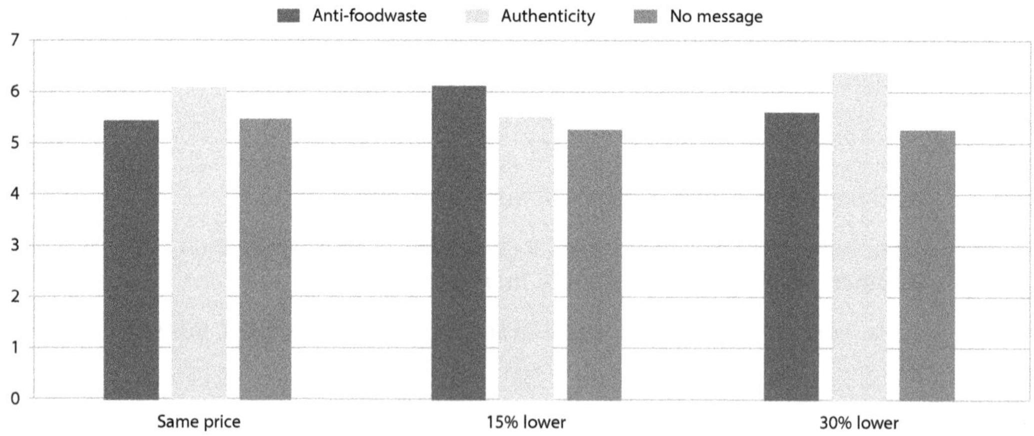

Source: ECORYS, Tilburg University and GfK (2015). © European Union, 2015. Reproduction is authorised provided the source is acknowledged.

Source

ECORYS, Tilburg University and GfK (2015), *Milan BExpo 2015 : A behavioural study on food choices and eating habits*, report for the European Commission, Brussels, http://dx.doi.org/10.2838/537411.

Annex 6.A3

Food waste and best-before/production dates – European Commission

Context	
Who?	Study developed by ECORYS, Tilburg University and GfK, ordered by the Consumers, Health, Agriculture and Food Executive Agency (CHAFEA) on behalf of the European Commission.
Where?	Universal Exposition, Milan, Italy.
When?	2015 (data collection between June 30 and July 6).
Why?	This lab experiment is part of a broader behavioural study tested consumer choices in relation to food sustainability. This intervention studied how the decision to use or dispose non-perishable long shelf-life food items is affected by the presence or absence of dates (e.g. production or best-before date) on food labelling.
Behavioural intervention	
Environmental policy objective	Incentivise environmentally sustainable consumption patterns.
Behavioural issue	Misinterpretation of "use by" and "best before" dates on food labelling and its impact on food waste at household level.
Behavioural lever	Simplification and framing of information.

Evaluation of the intervention: methodology

Relevant population: Visitors of the Milan 2015 Universal Exposition.

Sample size and sampling method(s): 500 participants (mostly Italian), randomly picked among visitors of the Exposition. Note that the sample is very limited both in size and in nationalities represented.

Method: lab experiment.

Participants were randomly assigned to one of 6 treatments. No control group was set up: the experiment was based on a between-subjects design.

Participants judged non-perishable long shelf-life food items labelled with either a best-before date, a production date or no date, where:

- best-before date (BBD): optimal quality guarantee;
- use-by date: date by which a product can be eaten safely (for highly perishable goods).

In addition, some participants evaluated non-perishable products with a perceived short shelf-life beyond the best-before date (pasta sauce and orange juice) and some with a perceived long shelf-life beyond the best-before date (coffee and pasta). A summary of the treatments is provided in Table 6.A3.1.

Table 6.A3.1. **Treatment allocation**

Treatment	BBD/no date/production date	Short/long shelf-life	Products (in randomised order)
1	BBD	Short	Juice, sauce
2	BBD	Long	Pasta, coffee
3	No date	Short	Juice, sauce
4	No date	Long	Pasta, coffee
5	Production date	Short	Juice, sauce
6	Production date	Long	Pasta, coffee

Source: ECORYS, Tilburg University and GfK (2015). © European Union, 2015. Reproduction is authorised provided the source is acknowledged.

For each of the two products they were shown, participants in this experiment were asked to indicate the following under four different scenarios (a substantial amount of time before the BBD, just before the BBD, just after the BBD, a substantial amount of time after the BBD):

a. their willingness to use/keep versus throw away a product,

b. their perceived product quality, and

c. their perceived product safety, at four different time points.

Units of measurement: Score relative to the various assessed variables (disposal probability, perceived product safety, perceived product quality) as stated by respondents, out of a proposed scale.

Findings

- Understanding of best-before dates: only 47% of experiment participants indicate the correct meaning.
- Disposal probability: consumers were asked to indicate how likely they were to dispose of a product being given a best-before date, a production date or no date, together with an indication of the approximate shelf life of the product relative to these significant dates.
- The authors underlined that "Overall, it is difficult to tell whether no date is preferred over best before date, because this strongly depends on how long consumers typically keep long shelf-life, non-perishable products in their cupboard before consuming them." (ECORYS, Tilburg University and GfK, 2015, p. 19)
- *Likelihood of disposing of products* increased across all time points whenever a production date was provided as opposed to no date at all. Showing a production date was shown to less effective (for products with long shelf-life) or equally effective (for products with short shelf-life) compared to showing no date information.
- When it came to *perceived product safety*, products labelled with a best-before date were perceived safer than similar goods with other marking up until the BBD was reached. After this time mark, there was evidence that showing no date mark was preferable over providing a best-before date or production date.

- *Perceived product quality*: before the best-before date is reached, presence of this date on products is connected to higher quality perceptions relatively to products without a date mark or products with a production date. After the best-before date is reached, providing no date mark is more effective than providing both a best-before date and a production date.

Source

ECORYS, Tilburg University and GfK (2015), *Milan BExpo 2015 : A behavioural study on food choices and eating habits*, report for the European Commission, Brussels, http://dx.doi.org/10.2838/537411.

Note

1. See http://ec.europa.eu/food/safety/food_waste/eu_actions/date_marking/index_en.htm (consulted on 20 September 2016).

Reference

ECORYS, Tilburg University and GfK (2015), *Milan BExpo 2015 : A behavioural study on food choices and eating habits*, report for the European Commission, Brussels, http://dx.doi.org/10.2838/537411.

Chapter 7

Using behavioural insights to improve waste management and resource efficiency

This chapter presents behavioural interventions implemented to improve waste management and resource efficiency policies. Relevant behavioural biases are highlighted, together with the behavioural levers used by policy makers to tackle them. On the one hand, there have been interventions trying to ensure sound waste management, e.g. preventing littering. On the other hand, a number of interventions promote the 3Rs (reduce, reuse, recycle), e.g. by inducing the purchase of long-living products and encouraging product repair as opposed to replacement.

Resource efficiency and waste management policies have multiple aims, which can be summarised with the 3Rs: reduce, reuse, recycle. Opting for longer-living products and packaging-free goods can, for instance, reduce waste generation. Eco-design can facilitate product reuse by simplifying repairs through modular components. Waste should be properly discarded and sorted (e.g. avoiding littering), incentivising the reuse and recycling of waste materials.

Multiple behavioural biases affect individual choices surrounding waste generation, sorting and recycling, as well as product reuse (see Reader's Guide for definitions of all technical terms):

- When it comes to product choice, consumers subject to *status-quo bias* will naturally opt for standard, default options: if repair services for broken mobile phones are not common, mobile phones will be more likely replaced with new ones instead of having their lifespan extended.
- Correct waste sorting and recycling is hindered by the often unintuitive design of waste bins. Their design is often the by-product of complex waste sorting regulations; thus, correctly sorting waste requires a conscious effort rather than an automatic, effortless act.
- Littering is influenced both by *attitude-behaviour gaps* (whereby individuals do not reckon correct waste disposal as necessary civic duty), by miscalculation of the consequences of littering (both personal, e.g. being fined, and public, e.g. generating an environmental externality in the form of unregulated dumpsites) and by negative *social norms* (whereby individuals can be "incentivised" to litter if they see everyone else doing so).

Alongside behavioural biases, various market features hinder the implementation of policies based on the 3Rs and make it difficult for consumers to minimise waste generation and to maximise reuse and recycling. At the product choice stage, there is obvious information asymmetry between producers and consumers regarding the expected lifespan of a product and its repair possibilities. When it comes to household waste generation, consumers rarely receive feedback regarding the amount and type of waste they generate. Furthermore, it may be complex to connect waste generation to the cost of waste collection, which may be billed to households by their municipality as part of a generic residence tax.

Behavioural insights can contribute to shaping resource efficiency and waste management policies in several ways. For example, a more intuitive design of recycling bins could ease household recycling efforts. Furthermore, making recycling more salient, e.g. through door-to-door waste collection in transparent trash bags, can help activate social norms in this context. When it comes to waste generation, providing feedback on the amount of waste produced – both in absolute terms and relatively to meaningful benchmarks – would make the cost and benefit of waste collection more salient, and could be paired with commitment devices.

Framing product lifespan information to foster the purchase of long-living products

Designing longer-living products or modular products (e.g. facilitating the replacement of malfunctioning components) can decrease waste. While there is asymmetric information between producers and consumers regarding product life expectancy, lifespan labelling can signal consumers the expected lifespan of a given product, thus possibly inducing a more resource efficient choice.

In 2016, the European Economic and Social Committee commissioned a study based on a stated choice experiment to assess to what extent consumers' product choices were affected by lifespan labelling. More specifically, the experiment tested four different visual displays of lifespan labels for 9 categories of products (suitcases, printers, trousers, sport shoes, coffee makers, washing machines, vacuum cleaners and smartphones) in four different geographical regions and under different product price scenarios (European Economic and Social Committee, 2016).

Participants in the experiment could select products from a simulated online retail platform. This behavioural intervention showed that, in spite of different displays, all lifespan labels led consumers to purchase products with a longer lifespan: on average, sales of long-living products increased by 13.8% relatively to shorter-living ones in the same class. Sales of all products but televisions were affected: this varied from 23.7% for suitcases to 11.4% for smartphones.

As suitcases are used for sporadic travels, they may be expected to last longer: this is the explanation associated with the large impact that lifespan labels have proven to have in driving the purchase of long-living suitcases. Conversely, the less important impact of such labels for smartphones may be due to the fact that consumers replace such devices relatively often, as technological improvements kick in leading to the development of better performing phones. The lack of a significant impact of labels on the purchase of televisions may be explained by the fact that the lifespan variation across the 10 television sets proposed may not have been sufficiently large to attract consumers' attention to this specific criterion.

Lifespan labels were shown to steer purchasing decisions towards longer-living products regardless of their price. However, it appeared that these labels had a more important impact on purchases of more expensive products (+15.3%) relatively to low-end ones (+14.1%). This is intuitive, as consumers bound to invest in an expensive durable good may want to make sure that it has a long lifetime.

From replacement to repair: changing default options to decrease electronic waste

As consumption of electronics increases, so does the amount of electronic waste requiring disposal. Correct disposal and recycling of the materials used in electronic goods is particularly important for minimising the environmental and health impacts associated with their extraction and disposal. While supply-side measures such as extended producer responsibility are crucial to ensure the engagement of producers in correct disposal of electronics, a study by the Nordic Council argues that there is ample room for demand-side measures (Stefansdotter et al., 2016). Such measures would leverage behavioural insights to tackle phenomena hindering the sustainable consumption of electronic goods. Examples of concrete measures are incentives to replace electronic goods less often, to opt for environmentally friendly or long-living models and to correctly recycle them if reuse is not an option.

The study recognises that the consumer's decision-making process in this respect differs according to the type of electronic good concerned (be it a mobile phone or a white good appliance), and the decision involved (decision to purchase, reuse or recycle). Furthermore, consumers belonging to different demographic groups may well have heterogeneous preferences when it comes to electronics. Considering the heterogeneity at play in this sector, the authors have chosen to focus on the consumption of mobile phones in the age-group 19-28 years old in the Nordic Countries.

The study included two phases. In the first one, a sample of young consumers was surveyed in a Danish electronics shop to identify unintended behaviours or behavioural obstacles preventing sustainable consumption of electronics throughout their entire lifecycle (e.g. identification of barriers to repairing broken devices instead of replacing them with new ones; barriers to purchases of second-hand goods). In the second phase, two stated choice experiments were carried out in order to test the impact of different treatments on mobile phone purchase decisions. Depending on the treatment group, slightly different hypothetical purchasing situations were described and participants were asked to answer a questionnaire indicating the actions they would take in the described circumstances.

The first experiment simulated the situation of having a broken mobile phone: in this context, consumers had to choose between buying a new phone or repairing the broken one in a scenario, and buying a new phone or buying a second-hand one in an alternative scenario. This experiment aimed at understanding if young consumers would be interested in reparation or second-hand possibilities, which are not automatically offered by electronics shops.

Results from the first scenario showed that 87% of consumers would opt for repairs if that option was offered in store (twenty percentage points more than in the baseline scenario where only new phones would be proposed). In the second scenario, 28.9% of consumers would opt for the second-hand mobile phone, this being 7 times more than in the baseline scenario. All these results were statistically significant.

The second experiment aimed at increasing the percentage of young people opting to lease their mobile as an alternative to buying it, by including a third, clearly undesirable option (e.g. a more expensive mobile leasing scheme). This led 62% of consumers to choose to lease their phone, as opposed to only 38% in the baseline scenario. A variation of this stated choice experiment explicitly stated that the mobile phone under consideration was "green", meaning its components were sourced respecting certain sustainability criteria: this intervention, however, did not yield any statistically significant result.

These results signal that young consumers are open to considering sustainable alternatives to the purchase of new mobile phones (e.g. repairing old phones, buying second-hand devices). However, these options have thus far been rarely offered in the mobile phone market, hindering the adoption of more sustainable behaviours. This expands the findings from the study on product lifespan information developed by the European Economic and Social Committee, showing that population subgroups may have different motivations towards the 3R objectives, and may thus respond differently to related behavioural interventions.

Leveraging social norms, salience and commitment devices to decrease littering

In 2010, eight municipalities in the Netherlands participated in a project aimed at reducing littering in the immediate surroundings of waste containers. The project was commissioned by the Foundation Nederland Schoon and Agentschap NL, a division of the Dutch Ministry of Economic Affairs at that time (Dijksterhuis & Van Baaren, Tabula Rasa and IPR Normag, 2010).

Six behavioural interventions were tested through a field experiment with a before/after design: in each treatment group, waste containers and their surroundings were monitored for two weeks (baseline), which were then followed by two weeks of treatment. The six rolled-out treatments were:

1. *Self-correction by self-reflection*: placing a mirror next to the waste container, so that people see themselves when bringing their waste to the container.

2. *Injunctive social norm*: placing a picture of a person littering next to waste containers alongside the request to behave in the right way by throwing trash bags in the appropriate containers.
3. *Descriptive social norm*: placing alongside the waste containers a sign with the text: "Help to keep it clean here: most people in this neighbourhood do not litter around the containers".
4. *Monitoring and penalties*: monitoring waste container sites and placing a warning that littering can result in a fine.
5. *Commitment and consistency*: the "foot-in-the-door" approach consists in first prompting people to a generic commitment (e.g. commit to keeping the neighbourhood clean) and then giving them a concrete hint of how to honour that commitment (e.g. placing a sign next to the container inviting them to keep the neighbourhood clean by not littering).
6. *Setting the right norm*: emptying the containers more frequently and keeping their location clean.

The experiment showed that three of the interventions had statistically significant effects. The descriptive social norm intervention led to a reduction in littering frequency from 50% to 30%; mechanisms based on monitoring and penalties resulted in a reduction from 51% to 29% and commitment devices led to a reduction from 45% to 28%. For the remaining interventions, no significant effect was found.

Green defaults to save resources

Because individuals are subject to status-quo bias, simplifying their daily effortful activities by changing default options to more environmentally sustainable ones can "green" routine behaviour without entailing additional effort on the part of consumers.

As its first annual report explains, throughout its first year of operation, the United States Social and Behavioural Sciences Team implemented a range of "proof-of-concept projects where behavioral insights could be embedded directly into programs at a low cost and lead to immediate, quantifiable improvements in program outcomes" (Social and Behavioral Sciences Team, 2015).

One such project was aimed at reducing the use of printing paper (and thus the costs of printing) at a Federal Government agency (US Department of Agriculture's Economic Research Service), testing whether the introduction of a green default could deliver these outcomes (see Annex 7.A1). Upon launching a print job, users were prompted to switch to double-sided printing: introducing this green default increased the likelihood of double-sided printing on a given print job by 5.8 percentage points from a baseline of 46%. This result prompted the agency to extend the green default to all its printers.

This field experiment provides an example of how public institutions themselves can "green" their procedures leveraging behavioural insights. More specifically, it shows the power of green defaults, which build upon consumer inertia to promote sustainable consumption choices.

Conclusion on waste management and resource efficiency

The behavioural insights applications to resource efficiency and waste management policies reviewed in this report have mainly relied on *framing and simplification of information* (e.g. product lifespan labelling) and on *changes to the physical environment* (e.g. signs describing correct waste disposal alongside waste collection points). While not many behavioural interventions have been implemented in this field, they have leveraged a variety of additional insights: *green defaults, use of social norms, feedback mechanisms,* and *commitment devices.*

Experiments aimed at ensuring efficient use of printing paper and of mobile phones have shown the way various behavioural levers, from green defaults to differently framed messages, can prompt consumers to reduce their waste generation by using or reusing a product to its full potential (Social and Behavioral Sciences Team, 2015). Lifespan labels have shown that product labelling does have the potential to impact consumer purchases by redirecting them towards lower-impact, more durable goods (European Economic and Social Committee, 2016). There is some evidence that leveraging social norms can also induce e.g. correct waste disposal (Dijksterhuis & Van Baaren et al., 2010).

While there has been considerable action involving interventions aimed at encouraging the reuse and repair of products, ultimately leading consumers to fully exploit their lifespan, there have not been any interventions aimed at reducing waste generation or at encouraging correct waste sorting at home. This may seem surprising, as indicators to track waste generation are potentially straightforward (e.g. volume, number of trash bags filled, weight). However, monitoring changes in these parameters is complex, as most waste is generated at home. Tracking sorting and recycling patterns is subject to the same constraint. The lack of transparency surrounding "waste choices" is likely the biggest obstacle to the application of behavioural insights to this policy area.

Annex 7.A1

Green printing defaults to save paper – United States

Context	
Who?	Department of Agriculture's (USDA) Economic Research Service (ERS), in collaboration with the Social and Behavioral Sciences Team (SBST)
Where?	Government agency offices, USA
When?	Unspecified
Why?	Test whether the introduction of a green printing default can reduce total paper use and printing costs at a Federal Government agency
Behavioural intervention	
Environmental policy objective	Encourage conservation of resources
Behavioural issue	Status quo bias
Behavioural lever	Change in the default policy

Evaluation of the intervention: methodology

Relevant population: Economic Research Service (ERS)'s employees.

Sample size and sampling method(s): Unspecified.

Method

This was a between-groups field experiment, in which the treatment was randomised at the printer level within ERS: different groups of users relying on different printers would be exposed to the treatment or not.

More specifically, the treatment involved changing the default printing option by introducing a small cost in terms of additional time associated with single-sided documents. Whenever employees initiated a single-sided print job, a dialog box would appear on their screen, prompting them to change their default printer setting to double-sided, but still allowing them to continue to single-printing if preferred.

Units of measurement: Percentage change in double-sided printing on a given print job.

Findings

Individuals who are exposed to the dialog box prompting them to switch to double-sided printing are more likely to print double-sided. This prompt increases the likelihood of double-sided printing on a given job by 5.8 percentage points ($p < 0.01$, 95% confidence interval [4.2, 7.4]), from a baseline of 46 percent. Note that on the basis of this result, ERS has decided to change the default settings of all of its printers to double-sided.

Source

Social and Behavioral Sciences Team (2015), *Social and Behavioral Sciences Team 2015 Annual Report*, Office of Science and Technology Policy, Washington, DC.

References

Dijksterhuis & Van Baaren, Tabula Rasa and IPR Normag (2010), *Voorbij Bijplaatsingen. Voorbij Bijplaatsingen Gedragsinterventies voor het effectief terugdringen van bijplaatsingen bij afvalcontainers*, report for Stichting Nederland Schoon and Agentschap NL.

European Economic and Social Committee (2016), *The influence of lifespan labelling on consumers*, Brussels.

Social and Behavioral Sciences Team (2015), *Social and Behavioral Sciences Team 2015 Annual Report*, Office of Science and Technology Policy, Washington, DC.

Stefansdotter, A. et al. (2016), *Nudging för hållbar konsumtion av elektronikprodukter (Nudging the sustainable consumption of electronic goods),* executive summary in English, report for the Nordic Council of Ministers, Copenhagen.

Chapter 8

Using behavioural insights to increase compliance with environmental regulation and participation in voluntary schemes

This chapter presents behavioural interventions implemented to increase compliance with environmental regulation and participation in voluntary schemes, both on the side of individuals and firms. The behavioural biases at play are highlighted, together with the behavioural levers used by policy makers to tackle them. Behavioural interventions have been rolled out both to increase firm compliance with reporting requirements, such as those on the import of environmentally harmful substances, to promote individual compliance with the payment of environmentally related fines, such as those on littering, and to make the uptake of "soft" policy instruments such as voluntary certification more appealing.

The statistical data for Israel are supplied by and under the responsibility of the relevant Israeli authorities. The use of such data by the OECD is without prejudice to the status of the Golan Heights, East Jerusalem and Israeli settlements in the West Bank under the terms of international law.

Behavioural insights applications reported thus far targeted individual behaviour. However, the employees responsible for taking action within firms in order to e.g. ensure compliance with relevant environmental standards may also be subject to standard behavioural biases (see Reader's Guide for definitions of all technical terms). For example, they may suffer from cognitive limitations preventing their full understanding of complex regulatory requirements. With limited information on the functioning of government monitoring and compliance check schemes, employees in regulated firms may be overconfident regarding the possibilities of their business being monitored, thus choosing to risk incurring a fine for non-compliance. Conversely, when it comes to the uptake of voluntary certifications, businesses may eschew it because of inertia, given such certifications may be perceived as not fully related to their core business. For these reasons, behavioural sciences can contribute to informing environmental policy making in order to increase firms' compliance with regulations or to encourage their uptake of voluntary schemes.

Sifting through the complexity of bureaucratic steps needed for firms to comply with environmental regulation can result into information overload, ultimately hindering compliance itself. Simplifying and reframing regulatory procedures and reporting requirements could ease the way, increasing compliance rates. Alongside such changes to "hard", mandatory environmental regulation, behavioural interventions could increase the uptake of "soft" environmental policy instruments such as voluntary certifications and standards. This could be achieved, for instance, by increasing the salience of the benefits associated with such decisions, framing the uptake of voluntary certifications and standards as an opportunity rather than a regulatory burden.

Increasing individual and business compliance with environmental regulation

Through its Design and Analytics Team, the *Australian Government Department of the Environment* has developed and run a field experiment aimed at *increasing reporting compliance among regulated entities* (see Annex 8.A1). The specific regulation under scrutiny requires entities with a licence to import equipment containing ozone-depleting substances and synthetic greenhouse gases to submit quarterly import reports to the Department of the Environment.

The objective of this randomised controlled trial was to increase the reporting compliance of licensed entities by incorporating behavioural insights techniques into reminder notification processes. This translated into changes in the design of reminder messages and their timing, rolled out throughout reporting periods between July 2014 and March 2015.

The experiment showed that the most effective intervention entailed i) a message with increased emphasis on reporting being mandatory, including a direct link to the online reporting system and three simple steps to get there, and ii) both an early and a last-minute reminder. This intervention delivered a 26% increase in compliance relative to the control group.

The same behavioural insights can be exploited to tackle the drivers of individual non-compliance with environmental regulation. For example, the *behavioural insights team at the Israeli Minister of Environmental Protection* is developing a before/after intervention by *reframing fines for littering* with the aim of increasing offenders' payment of the fines. The letter communicating the infraction has been redesigned and rewritten following some of the best practices suggested by the UK Behavioural Insights Team (Behavioural Insights Team, 2015): personalising the message, simplifying the language, highlighting key actions to be taken in order to pay the fine, as well as the consequences of not paying in time (leveraging loss aversion). The redesigned letter also tries to nudge altruistic reactions, by highlighting the fact that revenues from fines fund environmental protection and conservation.

This intervention is still ongoing, hence its results have not been empirically assessed yet. However, it is worth mentioning that this project has prompted the construction of a database allowing the systematic collection and analysis of data on fines issued and paid. This is an excellent example of the positive spill-overs that behavioural interventions can generate through their focus on impact evaluation: in this case, the introduction of systematic data analysis practices in procedures monitoring compliance with environmental regulation.

Investigating businesses' motivations in participating in voluntary schemes

The objective of this field experiment, launched by the *Australian Government Department of the Environment*, was to understand *businesses' motivations for becoming voluntarily certified as carbon neutral* (see also Annex 8.A2 for further information on the Carbon Neutral Program and on the experiment itself).

This randomised controlled trial tested the impact of priming messages on businesses' interests in different marketing messages. Participants at a carbon emissions reduction summit were verbally primed with one of two messages before being asked if they would like to receive more information on the environmental benefits and/or competitive advantages of being certified as carbon neutral. The first priming message focused on intrinsic motivation, emphasising the environmental benefits of being certified as carbon neutral; the other message focused on extrinsic motivation, emphasising the competitive advantages for a business certified as carbon neutral.

Following the verbal priming, all participants were asked to complete a postcard with their details. The postcard prompted participants to signal whether they would like to receive further information on the Program, and if so, what information specifically they would like to receive (e.g. how a carbon neutral certification can give businesses a competitive edge, help them retain staff or lead the way towards a low carbon economy).

Overall findings indicated that summit participants were unwilling to request information on the competitive advantages of going carbon neutral if the marketing messages they had received only highlighted the intrinsic, environmental benefits of doing so.

Conclusion on compliance with environmental regulation and participation in voluntary schemes

Evidence from applications of behavioural insights to increase both environmental compliance with mandatory environmental regulation and uptake of voluntary environmental certification and standards comes entirely from field experiments based on the simplification and framing of information.

Emphasising the mandatory nature of reporting duties and simplifying and increasing the salience of required steps for compliance has been shown to increase firms' regulatory compliance in Australia. Reminders sent out at key moments have also proven to be effective. The same insights are being leveraged in Israel in order to increase the payment of littering fines.

Evidence from Australia shows that, when approached with different priming messages regarding the uptake of carbon neutral voluntary certification, firms did not inquire about the potential competitive advantages connected to it unless prompted to do so. This may signal a lack of understanding of the concrete benefits connected to certification uptake, or a wish to focus on environmental consequences.

Annex 8.A1

Increasing compliance with reporting obligations – Australia

Context	
Who?	The Australian Government Department of the Environment
Where?	Australia
When?	July to September 2014 (reporting period 1) October to December 2014 (reporting period 2) January 2015 to March 2015 (reporting period 3)
Why?	Entities with a licence to import equipment containing ozone-depleting substances and synthetic greenhouse gases must submit quarterly import reports to the Department of the Environment. Entities are required to report under the *Ozone Protection and Synthetic Greenhouse Gas Management Act 1989.* This legislation helps to ensure Australia meets its legal obligations under the Montreal Protocol on Substances that Deplete the Ozone Layer and the United Nations Framework Convention on Climate Change. The objective of the intervention was to increase the reporting compliance of licensed entities by incorporating behavioural insights into reminder notification processes.
Behavioural intervention	
Environmental policy objective	Increase compliance with environmental regulation
Behavioural issue	Cognitive limitations preventing employees in licensed entities (firms) from fully understanding complex regulatory requirements; overconfidence and underestimation of the risk of being fined for non-compliance.
Behavioural lever	Simplification and framing of information

Evaluation of the intervention: methodology

Relevant population: Entities with a current licence to import equipment containing ozone-depleting substances and synthetic greenhouse gases into Australia.

Sample size and sampling method(s): The sample size was 667 licensed entities.

Method: Field experiment designed as randomised controlled trial.

Licensed entities were randomly assigned to one of 5 groups (one control group and 4 treatment groups, with around 133 members per group), ensuring that all entities in all groups had similar levels of experience with the reporting process.

To help ensure this, a "poor compliance" variable was created using data collected during the three reporting periods prior to the start of the trial. Entities that were late in reporting in two of the three periods were regarded to have a poor compliance record.

The different groups were exposed to the following interventions:

- *Control group*: standard e-mail reminder notification already in use by the Department.

- *E-mail redesign 1*: this treatment utilised bright colour, a large photo banner, simple language and simple instructions, and a big "Lodge your report here" button.
- *E-mail redesign 2*: this treatment replaced the photo with the Government crest and increased emphasis on reporting being mandatory. It also included a new hyperlink to a different web page fewer "clicks" away from the online reporting portal along with instructions guiding recipients to the reporting portal.
- *E-mail redesign 2 paired with an early reminder.*
- *E-mail redesign 2 paired with both an early and a last-minute reminder.*

Units of measurement: Percentage change in compliance (in-time reporting) compared to the control group.

Findings

The trial results indicated that entities with a poor compliance record were almost 50 per cent less likely to report on time than other entities.

Analysis of data over three reporting periods found the results reported in Table 8.A1.1.

Table 8.A1.1. **Results by treatment group**

Treatment group	Description of treatment received	Reporting period in which treatment was received	Percentage increase in compliance (%)	Statistical significance
1	E-mail redesign 1	1, 2 and 3	6	Not significant
2	E-mail redesign 2	2 and 3	11	p<0.01
3	E-mail redesign 2, paired with an early reminder	3	10	p<0.03
4	E-mail redesign 2, paired with both an early and a last-minute reminder	3	26	p<0.01

Treatment groups 3 and 4 were both exposed to multiple behavioural interventions. In addition, in the second reporting period, all groups received an early reminder in accordance with departmental practice prior to the combined Christmas and summer holiday period in Australia. There is evidence that the most effective intervention was e-mail redesign 2, paired with both an early and a last-minute reminder, leading to a 26% percentage increase in in-time reporting.

The cost of this intervention is minimal compared to the savings that result from increased compliance. A 26% increase in compliance means 180 fewer non-compliant entities to follow up each quarter. If half of these entities report immediately after receiving a late reminder e-mail and the Department makes a five-minute phone call to the other half, the Program would gain around 15 hours of staff time per quarter, or 60 hours per year. The Department would also save the telecommunications costs associated with making these calls.

Source

Information retrieved from e-mail exchanges with the Australian Government Department of the Environment.

Annex 8.A2

Investigating businesses' motivations in becoming certified as carbon neutral – Australia

Context	
Who?	The Australian Government Department of the Environment
Where?	Melbourne, Australia
When?	May 2-3, 2016
Why?	The Australian Government's Carbon Neutral Program allows organisations, products, services and events to be certified as carbon neutral against the National Carbon Offset Standard. This means that net associated emissions are equal to zero. Certified organisations, products, services and events are permitted to use the National Carbon Offset Standard trade mark. The standard sets minimum requirements for calculating, auditing and offsetting the carbon account of an organisation, product, service or event to voluntarily achieve carbon neutrality, and provides guidance on what is a genuine offset unit. The standard is voluntary but businesses must verify that they have complied with the minimum requirements to become certified. The objective of the intervention was to investigate businesses' motivations in becoming certified as carbon neutral, by testing the impact of priming messages on businesses' interests in different marketing messages.
Behavioural intervention	
Environmental policy objective	Increase compliance with environmental regulation
Behavioural issue	Status quo bias
Behavioural lever	Simplification and framing of information

Evaluation of the intervention: methodology

Relevant population: Participants at the 3rd Annual Emissions Reduction Summit, Melbourne, Australia.

Sample size and sampling method(s): Convenience sample of N = 48.

Method: Field experiment designed as a randomised controlled trial.

Participants at a carbon emissions reduction summit were randomly assigned either to the control group or to one of the two treatment groups based on the time of day (motivating messages were changed hourly):

- *Priming message 1*: intrinsic motivation emphasising the environmental benefits of being certified carbon neutral.
- *Priming message 2*: extrinsic motivation emphasising the competitive advantages for a business certified as carbon neutral.
- *Control group*: default marketing message.

All participants were primed with one of the two messages, with roughly equal numbers of participants being exposed to each message. Following the verbal priming, all participants were asked to complete a postcard with their details. The postcard prompted participants to signal whether they would like to receive further information on the Program, and if so, what information specifically they would like to receive. The following four options were given:

"Yes, please send me information about how going carbon neutral can (please tick one):

- *Give my business a competitive edge.*
- *Support my business to attract and retain the best staff.*
- *Showcase my business as leading the way towards a low carbon economy.*
- *Show that my business is certified carbon neutral with credible and robust standards."*

The order of the four options was randomised between participants.

Units of measurement: The number of instances that participants requested more information on specific marketing messages.

Findings

Participants that received priming messages emphasising the competitive advantages related to carbon neutral certification were more likely to request further written information on such advantages. Conversely, participants that received priming messages emphasising the environmental benefits of carbon neutrality did not show any preference for receiving one type of written information over another. The statistical significance was not assessed due to small samples sizes.

Source

Information retrieved from e-mail exchanges with the Australian Government Department of the Environment.

Reference

Behavioural Insights Team (2015), *The Behavioural Insights Team Update Report 2013-2015*, Behavioural Insights Ltd., London.

ORGANISATION FOR ECONOMIC CO-OPERATION AND DEVELOPMENT

The OECD is a unique forum where governments work together to address the economic, social and environmental challenges of globalisation. The OECD is also at the forefront of efforts to understand and to help governments respond to new developments and concerns, such as corporate governance, the information economy and the challenges of an ageing population. The Organisation provides a setting where governments can compare policy experiences, seek answers to common problems, identify good practice and work to co-ordinate domestic and international policies.

The OECD member countries are: Australia, Austria, Belgium, Canada, Chile, the Czech Republic, Denmark, Estonia, Finland, France, Germany, Greece, Hungary, Iceland, Ireland, Israel, Italy, Japan, Korea, Latvia, Luxembourg, Mexico, the Netherlands, New Zealand, Norway, Poland, Portugal, the Slovak Republic, Slovenia, Spain, Sweden, Switzerland, Turkey, the United Kingdom and the United States. The European Union takes part in the work of the OECD.

OECD Publishing disseminates widely the results of the Organisation's statistics gathering and research on economic, social and environmental issues, as well as the conventions, guidelines and standards agreed by its members.

OECD PUBLISHING, 2, rue André-Pascal, 75775 PARIS CEDEX 16
(97 2017 07 1 P) ISBN 978-92-64-27386-3 – 2017

www.ingramcontent.com/pod-product-compliance
Ingram Content Group UK Ltd.
Pitfield, Milton Keynes, MK11 3LW, UK
UKHW051504290926
15471UKWH00008B/1408

9 789264 273863